# OUR STORY:
# 100% OFFICIAL

**New York • London**

# Quercus

Quercus
New York • London

Copyright © 2016 Bradley Simpson, James McVey, Connor Ball, Tristan Evans

The right of Bradley Simpson, James McVey, Connor Ball, Tristan Evans to be identified as the Authors of the Work has been asserted by them in accordance with the Copyright, Designs and Patents Act 1988.

First published in the United States in 2016 by Quercus

ISBN 978-1-68144-153-5

Library of Congress Control Number: 2016949790

Designed by Well Made Studio
All photography © Dean Sherwood, except:
Pages 3, 22 © Diana Gomez
Pages 69, 95, 124, 152, 168 © Andrew Whitton
Page 178 © Chris Jackson / Getty Images Entertainment

Printed and bound in Germany by Mohn Media

This book was printed on papers that are natural, renewable and recyclable products and made from wood grown in sustainable forests. The logging and manufacturing processes conform to the environmental regulations of the country of origin.

Distributed in the United States and Canada by
Hachette Book Group
1290 Avenue of the Americas
New York, NY 10104

10 9 8 7 6 5 4 3 2 1

www.quercus.com

# CONTENTS

MEET THE VAMPS

WHO WE ARE, HOW IT ALL HAPPENED, AND HOW CONNOR VERY NEARLY WASN'T IN THE BAND (SERIOUSLY)

**JAMES:** It all started back in 2011 when one of our managers, Richard Rashman, contacted me via MySpace after seeing some of the music I'd posted. He told me he'd put together Busted and McFly and that he was interested in putting a band together around me.

At that point I was doing quite a lot of solo acoustic gigs and really enjoying it, so I wasn't sure I wanted to be in a band. Plus, all the other people I knew who were in bands were out drinking and partying a lot, and I didn't want to be a part of that scene. I've never been the type to go out and get wasted.

After thinking it over for a while I decided I had nothing to lose so I swallowed my pride and called Richard back to hear more about what he wanted to do.

Richard explained that he was looking in the UK and America for more band members and he wanted me to see if I could find any talented guys off my own bat. The idea of putting a band together was quite daunting, but I always love a challenge!

I looked through a lot of videos of singers on YouTube – some amazing, some slightly scary – and I found a couple of guys who looked like they'd be a good fit. I'd never written with anyone but we met up and worked on some ideas, which was great because it helped to build up my confidence.

I ended up meeting loads of different people in the following six months after school and at weekends. And while everyone was really nice, there was no one I really clicked with musically.

Then, one night, I saw a video of Brad on YouTube singing an Ed Sheeran cover and I thought he had such an incredible voice. I also thought he looked about thirteen.

**BRAD:** I'm still not sure whether I'm flattered or insulted by that?

**JAMES:** It's a compliment! Anyway, I sent a link to the video to Richard and he came back and said he thought I should contact him. I tracked Brad down on Facebook and sent him a message explaining the project, and it must have seemed like the most random thing

ever. 'Hi, you don't know me, but would you like to be in a band with me?' Brad didn't reply and I didn't think he was interested. But then, three weeks later, Brad got in touch to say he was interested.

BRAD: I did think it was well weird, to be fair.

JAMES: I contacted Brad in late 2011 and we met up after chatting and messaging a lot. I went up to Birmingham to stay with him for the weekend, and it was the first time I'd travelled all that way on my own. I remember coming out of the train station and Brad came up to me. My first thought was, 'He's so small and he looks so young!'

It was quite a scary thing to do but luckily his family were really friendly towards me and made me feel so welcome. Brad even brought me pancakes in bed on the first morning. He'd never do that now. I can't think of anything he's *less* likely to do.

BRAD: I honestly can't believe I did that. It's like my body was taken over by aliens for the weekend. Every time we talk about that weekend it totally sounds like I was trying to woo James. It's very weird. Although he did also get caught up in the middle of a family argument.

My family and I had just been away to Barbados for a holiday and taken a load of photos. I think I'd been in trouble with my mum for something so I thought I'd make it up to her by skating into Sutton with the memory card and getting some of the pictures printed off. Only when I took the memory card out it had snapped in half and there was *nothing* they could do to recover it.

My sister was so angry with me, and then when I told my mum what had happened she got really upset and a bit of a row broke out (my family never argue so it was pretty bad). Poor James had to stand by while we had a family argument about me ruining all our holiday photos. That was one of his first impressions of the Simpson household, poor lad.

JAMES: I felt so awkward and really bad for them all. I was sat there wondering if I should go home, but Brad wouldn't hear of it.

Pancakes and arguments aside, we genuinely worked hard and came up with a couple of good songs, including a track called 'Rough Night'. We ended up putting the demo out later down the line because we really wanted people to hear what the first song we ever wrote was like, and it's since become a fan favourite.

Brad sang a song I'd written a couple of years before called 'Move My Way', which totally came to life when he performed it. I sent the songs to Richard and he came back straight away and said he really liked them. Whenever I'd sent him songs in the past he'd said they were 'OK', but this time he was really enthusiastic about what we'd done.

There was definitely songwriting chemistry and a real shared work ethic between me and Brad. We were both at school and had the same kind of commitments, and that made things easier too. We'd both go to school during the week and then meet up at the weekends to song write.

We were also both into skateboarding and playing *FIFA* and *Call of Duty*, and even though there were two school years between us – which is quite a lot when you're that age – we got on from the word go.

**TRISTAN:** And then I came along, which was obviously incredible.

**JAMES:** Yes, and then there was Tristan! He randomly added me on Facebook because we had a mutual friend who I'd written with before, and Tristan had been working with him too.

I had a look at Tristan's profile and saw that he was my age, good-looking and a drummer. I YouTubed him and watched him taking part in the 'Young Drummer of the Year' competition and he was so good.

It all felt a bit awkward because of our friend, but I asked Tristan if he wanted to come and write with Brad and me to see if we gelled.

**TRISTAN:** I wasn't sure what to do, but I knew that I wasn't very well suited musically to the friend I was playing with at the time, and it was such an amazing opportunity. It would have been crazy not to at least meet the guys.

Brad and I got the train down to James's house in Bournemouth together. James was wearing chinos when he picked us up from the station, and I'd gone to buy some just for the occasion to impress him because I'd seen that he was wearing them in his Facebook picture. I was more into coloured jeans at that time (you'll no doubt hear about the amazing red ones I was wearing) but I wanted to fit in.

We jammed together and it just worked. It felt like we were all on the same page and no one had any kind of ego. We all wanted the same things and we weren't just three guys who quite fancied getting a band together; we were actually going to do it.

**JAMES:** We put together a couple of songs on my Mac and sent them to Richard. Richard wasn't sure we needed a drummer at that point, but as soon as I met Tristan I knew he was a perfect fit. I also showed Richard a picture of the three of us together, and he could see that it worked.

**BRAD:** Tristan and I bonded straight away and I thought he was so funny. We shared a bed at James's house the first night and we topped and tailed. We were up all night laughing and making a noise so James's mum wouldn't let us share a bed again the next night. Terrible behaviour.

I remember when Tristan and James were staying at my house once. James went to bed early and Tristan and I carried on playing darts with loud music on. Then my parents came in from a night out and they were a bit drunk so we were all messing about. Suddenly I got a text from James asking us to keep the music down. You would have thought my parents would be the ones to send a text like that, not him. We probably were *quite* annoying.

**CON:** Listening to all of this is making me feel a bit jealous because I didn't join the band until much later on.

**TRISTAN:** Sorry, Con, but it is better now you're in the band, honest. Who else would I go on mad nights out with?

Brad and James told me all about Richard on that trip, and I was so impressed that he'd created McFly and Busted because they were my idols when I was younger.

The first time I spoke to Richard he called my parents' home phone. My dad answered and when he heard this American dude on the other end of the line he was really confused. And probably a little bit worried. But Richard really put his (and my) mind at rest.

I knew Richard lived in a hotel in London but I didn't know much else, and I didn't meet him until a couple of months down the line. He had no online presence whatsoever so I wasn't able to find out any more about him other than what the lads had told me and what I'd found out in our phone call, so I was quite nervous. But it was actually fine and he was a really cool guy.

**BRAD:** Before Connor (BC) we were three guys who were playing music acoustically who wanted to be really successful. We wanted to show the band to the world, but at that point we still didn't really know what The Vamps' sound was going to be, so we started recording covers while we worked on our own music.

**TRISTAN:** Brad, James and I wrote together a lot, and at the same time we began posting our covers on YouTube and they started getting crazy views. At the beginning we covered songs we heard on the radio and liked, and then we started reading comments and took requests.

The first song that was requested was One Direction's 'Live While We're Young', and that was filmed by a videographer called Dean Sherwood, who Richard introduced us to. That was a turning point for us because it looked really professional and it got over a million views. We were so happy.

We still work with Dean now and he films pretty much every video you'll ever see of us. He's the man.

**JAMES:** We recorded a mixture of songs we liked, and songs people asked for, but we only did songs we could put a unique take on. We didn't want to do covers that sounded the same as the original. What was the point in that? We looked at what Boyce Avenue were doing and took a lot of inspiration from them.

In the end we realised that if people liked our covers, they might well like our original songs too. There was a point where we were worried

we'd always be seen as a cover band because we'd seen other bands try to cross over and have a problem, but all we could do was hope for the best.

**BRAD:** After working together for about nine months we felt like we knew exactly how we wanted the band to be and we'd written a lot of songs we were really proud of. Richard said he wanted to start looking for a record deal for us, and that's when it hit us all that this was an actual 'thing'.

It was strange when we started shopping around for labels because that's when everything became really serious and we weren't just three lads having a laugh together any more. It was proper work time.

In such a short time I went from playing in front of 150 people at a gig to doing a showcase for record company people who could potentially completely change the course of my life.

**JAMES:** Richard made sure that getting our record deal was never a stress to us. He told us to focus on writing music and being the best musicians we can be, and he'd take care of the rest.

We wrote four songs to showcase to record labels, and then Richard set up meetings with them. We spent a couple of weeks being shopped to labels, as it's called, and we got a couple of offers in the first week. When we got that first offer it was amazing because we'd got to the point we'd dreamed of.

**BRAD:** The showcases involved us playing to different A&R guys (basically, the guys who can give you a record deal) in hotel rooms and record label offices, and each one seemed to be scarier than the last.

We met one guy called Joe Kentish from Mercury Records who we were convinced liked us the least out of everyone. He watched us with a pretty stern look on his face and didn't seem overly impressed.

The day after Kentish met us at the hotel he came back to see us perform again with Jason Iley, who was the president of Mercury Records. That's when we knew they were really serious. They invited us to play for around forty people at the label the following week, which was amazing but intense.

After initially not thinking Kentish was our biggest fan, funnily enough Mercury were the label we ended up signing with because they really understood the band and Kentish and Jason were so enthusiastic about what we were doing.

Kentish oversaw our entire first album, along with a lady called Rachel Paley, who really believed in us.

Coming from Birmingham, London felt like a big, scary place to me. And although I loved the buzz of it and it's got so much going on musically, I didn't know many people at the start of the band. Kentish and Rachel were great during that time and we became really good mates.

**JAMES:** We made our choice based on the people we met, regardless of how big or small the company was. The deals were all similar but Kentish totally got the band and knew we just wanted to make music.

We were worried that record companies would try and change us. We were just three young lads with very little experience. We wanted to be a part of something new and exciting that had legs, and we were really open to anything so I guess in some ways it would have been

easy for some record company bigwigs to mould us into whatever they wanted. But Mercury didn't show any signs of doing that. From the word go they let us be completely ourselves.

When you listen to our first album, *Meet The Vamps*, there are quite a lot of genres mixed in, and that's because the record label allowed us to experiment and explore new types of music. Some of the other record labels were great, but we wanted to work with a group of people who liked and supported us just as we were.

It was strange because getting signed was always our goal, but the hard work *really* started after that. I thought the real work went into actually getting a deal, but I was so wrong. We've been signed for three years now and we're working harder than ever.

Signing a record deal opened a door to a load of other rooms, and all of them contained hard work and commitment. But we were ready for it. I honestly think if I stayed solo I probably would have carried on for another year and then given up, and I have no idea what I'd be doing right now. I feel incredibly lucky.

**BRAD:** We got signed in November 2012 and Connor entered the picture just afterwards. We knew we really wanted a bass player (well, some of us did) to develop The Vamps further. We felt like we were limiting ourselves with two acoustic guitars and a drum and we wanted a bigger sound.

We auditioned a handful of guys and we saw some real shockers. There was one guy whose mum was clearly pushing him to do it. He told us all he'd only come along because she'd made him and all he wanted to do was play football.

We saw about five bassists in all but none of them felt right. One of them was boasting about how far he'd got with girls, and we did not need to know that stuff! Some of the guys already had egos and wanted to be the front man, so they were never going to work.

**TRISTAN:** I won't lie; I was really strongly against getting a fourth member at the point. I don't know why, it just didn't feel right to me.

James, Brad and I had bonded and we were sounding really good so I didn't get why they wanted to bring someone else in. I emailed Richard and Joe (our other manager Joe O'Neill, who we'll talk about a lot in this book) with my thoughts but for some reason – and I still don't know why – I copied in five high-up people from the record company as well. Richard and Joe weren't very happy because it made them look a bit unsure about the project.

The email was like a proper essay but I really wanted to get my point across. I liked the idea of being different and being a threesome like Blink 182 and Green Day. Rixton and 5SOS were already out there, and I didn't want to be too similar to them.

**JAMES:** Brad and I were still really set on bringing in a bassist, and we stumbled across Connor singing covers of Blink 182 on YouTube. He looked really young but when we looked him up on Facebook it said he was eighteen so we initially thought he was too *old*.

We were after a younger guy for the band who was around fifteen or sixteen and could be a Dougie from McFly type. We were going to carry on looking around but Richard said he wanted to speak to him first.

When Richard called him he admitted he was only sixteen, but he'd lied so he could get followers on Facebook.

TRISTAN: The first time we met Con was at the Royal Garden Hotel. He came in wearing a hoodie looking really nervous. He was the shyest dude ever, and now he's the funniest guy I know.

He played a cover of Ed Sheeran's 'Lego House' for us and Richard made him stop halfway through and start again while looking into everyone's eyes.

CON: That was *so* horrible. But while it sounds creepy, Richard was just doing it to see if I could perform for people and project like you need to be able to do in a band. Apparently Richard does that to everyone.

I stayed over in London that night and Brad and I shared a hotel room. We just sat and watched football and chatted to each other. I found out later that Tristan and James had been too scared to share with me because they didn't know me and thought it would be awkward.

The following day we had a board meeting with Mercury. I'd never even been in a record company let alone in a big meeting like that. I was also only there as a 'guest' because although Richard had told me I was the number one candidate for the band, nothing was confirmed until much later.

JAMES: I think Tris and I were a bit scared to share a hotel room with Con because he was so *quiet*. When we first met him he hardly spoke at all.

He was obviously really talented and we all wanted him in the band, but we were worried about how shy he was. We thought it might be a bit overwhelming for him because it can be pretty full-on.

A short while later Con came down to Tristan's house in Devon to record a few songs, but still not as a member of The Vamps. We were still working out if he'd definitely be right, so put a cover of Justin Bieber's 'All Around the World' up on YouTube to gauge the fans' reaction. Needless to say, the fans loved him and wanted him to be a member of The Vamps.

**CON:** I didn't go to the toilet for four days at Tristan's because I didn't want to give a bad impression. I was in proper pain. I was also in bed all the time because I can sleep through everything.

Everyone else would be down having breakfast and I wouldn't wake up until lunchtime. The other boys didn't feel like they knew me well enough to say anything though. Looking back, I'm shocked they still let me in the group after that.

**BRAD:** It was when we were in a studio in Shoreditch the following February recording with Nick Hodgson – who was the drummer in the Kaiser Chiefs – that we decided we officially wanted Connor to join the band.

Con went to the toilet (he'd clearly got over his phobia by then) and while he was gone we recorded a message on one of the tracks. When he came back we said, 'Con, what do you think to this bit?' and played him a tape of us saying, 'Will you be our bassist?' We videoed it and put it on YouTube and it was hilarious.

Once he got used to us and vice versa it was like he'd always been in the band. It must have been hard joining when we all knew each other well but he settled in so quickly.

He slowly started coming out of his shell a lot more and all of our personalities mixed really well. We're all genuinely best mates now.

**CON:** It's so scary to think that if Richard hadn't got in touch with me I could have ended up not being in the band. My life could be completely different now. I'd still be studying music tech and trying to get into a band.

I haven't watched the video of the guys asking me to be in the band yet because it makes me feel nervous for some reason, but I definitely will one day.

Literally a couple of months after I formally joined The Vamps we went on tour with McFly. It was completely crazy. What a way to get introduced to the band!

I guess I didn't get much of a chance to settle in before we went out on the road, but we were together constantly so it was a good crash course in properly getting to know each other.

**TRISTAN:** We rehearsed for the tour at my house in Devon. We were holed up in my garage for three days and that was a real turning point for us all because we were getting to know how things worked with Con in the band. And once he joined I knew I'd been wrong and we totally worked as a four-piece.

We had a few songs but we hadn't released that much at that point so we had to try and get everything ready pretty quickly. This was our big chance.

**JAMES:** When we found out we were doing the tour it was just *insane*. We watched DVDs of other live performances and we started creating our own stage style. We'd be in Tris's garage jumping around to no one, trying to imagine what it might be like to actually be there.

Going on 'The Best of McFly' tour was unbelievable. We'd always really looked up to them, and for our first proper show as a band we played for 3,000 people at the Oasis leisure centre in Swindon.

We rounded off the tour at Wembley and it was so exciting for us because it's such a legendary venue. We only played four songs but to this day it's still one of our most memorable gigs because it was the first time we performed there.

By the time we got to London a lot of the crowd had watched our performances from previous shows on YouTube so they were singing along to our songs, which felt amazing.

**BRAD:** The tour was incredible, and afterwards we started gearing up to release our first single, 'Can We Dance', which we'd already recorded in New York.

We arranged to play a gig at Westfield shopping centre in West London on 3 August to promo the song and we had no idea how many people would turn up. We'd just hoped *some* would. We had 250,000 subscribers on YouTube by that point, but we didn't know if that meant anyone would make the effort to actually come and see us.

The morning of the gig someone from Westfield phoned our record company and said that girls had been camping outside since 5 a.m. and they wanted to cancel the event because they didn't have enough security for it. It was crazy.

TRISTAN: In the end they allowed the gig to go ahead and the atmosphere was amazing. It really felt like we were starting to get somewhere.

The following day we travelled up to Glasgow for the first date of our fan rally, which was basically a mini tour we organised so we could perform to a load of new fans.

Again, we didn't know whether anyone would actually be there, but when we got to the venue there were hundreds of fans waiting outside and it was a huge shock. It was the first time we'd experienced proper hysteria and it really got to Brad. He was feeling unsure about this strange new world, and as the lead singer he was feeling a lot of pressure.

BRAD: I think it was a combination of tiredness and stress, and I felt really overwhelmed and panicky. Our other manager, Joe, was sitting in the dressing room with me and I was crying on and off for ages. I felt like The Vamps were finally becoming real and I didn't know if I could handle it.

We'd been away from home for a while and I guess I was missing normal life as well. It felt like something big was starting that was going to pull us away from everything we'd been used to and relied on for stability. It was like there was a massive weight on my shoulders and once we started on this road there was no way of jumping back off it again.

We'd just been a group of lads having a laugh up until that point, and then all of a sudden we were performing for loads of people and we had to be good. We *had* to be if we wanted the band to take off in the way we wanted it to. We weren't messing around in Tristan's garage any more, and we weren't supporting another band. All those fans were there for *us*.

Someone came and told us the venue doors were opening and people were coming in. The dressing room was quite quiet when the door was closed, but when someone opened it, it sounded like a million girls were chanting, 'WE WANT THE VAMPS!'

People kept coming in trying to help me and calm me down, but every time they went in and out of the dressing room the door would open and I'd hear the screaming again. I honestly thought I was going to be sick. The other lads were comforting me but they must have been almost as terrified as I was.

In the end I knew I had no choice but to go out and perform. There was no way we could let all those people down. All the boys gave me a hug and I took some deep breaths, and then I walked down the corridor, up the back steps and onto the stage.

There were loads of flashes going off and I felt so light-headed I wondered how the hell I was going to sing. But then the adrenalin kicked in and as soon as the first song kicked off something took over and I felt something different – *excitement*.

The show went really well in the end. I think because we'd been so nervous we just went for it, and once I got off stage I was totally fine again. It turned out what my head had been imagining backstage was a lot worse than actually performing.

TRISTAN: We were all really up for it during that show in the end, and at one point I jumped off stage and nearly hit Joe in the face. I think we were just so relieved we'd got through it, and after that the rest of the fan rallies felt comparatively easy and we actually really enjoyed them.

We shot the video for 'Can We Dance' later the same month in Guildford. The shoot went on through the night and at one point the police turned up. The lights from the set were so bright air traffic control had asked them to look into it because they were getting complaints from planes flying in.

Brad also had to do his first stage kiss on that video, which he wasn't hugely keen on ...

**BRAD:** It was weird because I was in a long-term relationship at that point. I spoke to my girlfriend first and she was fine about it, but I didn't realise how big the video was going to go. It seemed like it was playing everywhere for a while, and right at the end there's 'the' scene I kiss a girl. I must admit I was really embarrassed about my parents seeing it.

I also had to hang upside down with Philadelphia cheese smeared on my cheek during the opening scene, so that a dog would come and lick my face. Luckily we did it in one take. He was a gorgeous dog but his breath wasn't great.

We weren't happy with what we were wearing in the video, and we found the director pretty scary. But overall the video shoot was a lot of fun.

Our friends came along, it was a nice day and we got to play football in between takes. We've got great memories of it, and when we look at every video we've shot now they remind us of really significant times in our lives.

**JAMES:** We were up at 4.30 a.m. to start shooting and we worked until 3 a.m. the following morning, so it was a long day. We sometimes do two-day shoots and they can be more relaxed because you're not so up against it time-wise.

**CON:** We went on a radio tour around the UK to support the single release. We'd turn up, chat on the radio, play some acoustic music and then go to the next venue. Hundreds of fans turned up to every station and we loved it.

**TRISTAN:** We went to Radio 1 for the first time to appear on Matt Edmonson's show, and that was a big deal for us. By that point we'd built up a good following on Twitter so we tweeted saying, 'If you're around, come and say hey.' We thought a few people might turn up, but over a thousand gathered outside and the security team were really worried so they told us off. To this day we're not supposed to tweet when we go into Radio 1. It's become a running joke with all the security there, and they always pretend they dread us going in.

**JAMES:** We went straight from there to an interview at Capital Radio in Leicester Square and we came out to over a thousand fans there too. They all surged forward and we couldn't get through them to get to our van, and Richard hurt his back in the crush. Of course the fans never meant to do any harm, and that taught us that we had to start having security with us. Nowadays we always make sure we have extra security so everyone is safe, especially the fans. We would be devastated if any of them got hurt.

We also had to do press interviews for the single and that was so weird. We were very normal guys from normal backgrounds and we weren't used to people trying to make us say certain things and catch us out.

It's quite a weird way of conversing and some of us were in relationships and weren't keen to talk about it, so that was tricky. But luckily everything that was written about us was positive and we got into the swing of it pretty quickly.

**CON:** We have read some weird stuff about ourselves over the years though. I once read I'd had a stroke in an online newspaper. And once one site writes something it can spread really quickly. I was also apparently dating Jade from Little Mix for a while, but neither of us was aware of it!

There was another rumour that Tristan and James had 700 shots each at a party, which is so ridiculous because they'd be dead now. They were only at the party for about seventeen minutes anyway, so that would have been fast work.

We're really lucky because we don't get papped privately though. If we go to an event of course we expect to have our photo taken, but we're never going to be one of those bands that try to have our picture taken coming out of a supermarket or go out of our way to get into the papers.

**JAMES:** Releasing our first single was strange because absolutely everything was new. If I'm being totally honest I wasn't that blown away with 'Can We Dance' when we first recorded it so I had no idea how it would do.

It was a good sign that people were turning up to see us when we did interviews, but we weren't a One Direction type of band who were coming off the back of a TV show. We were releasing a single off the back of our YouTube fan base.

It was the fans who built up a buzz so that radio companies played our single, and they also started networking around the world. They were incredible.

**TRISTAN:** It was really exciting finally getting our music out there but the build-up was ridiculous and we were very scared. We'd done the McFly tour, the summer shows, the radio and the fan rallies. We'd put in the work but we didn't know if that would have a bearing on the chart position. We had to play a really horrible waiting game.

**BRAD:** The single was released on 29 September and it went in at number one the same day. We were all in a massive state of shock. How the charts worked back then was that you'd find out your chart position based on iTunes orders and pre-sales on a Monday, and then you get a position every day until Friday. But after Friday you have to wait until Sunday to find out your final chart position. We were over a thousand copies ahead of OneRepublic's 'Counting Stars' on the Friday, but they kept creeping ever closer ...

**JAMES:** It felt like the longest week of our lives and we were gutted when we found out we missed out on the number one spot by a thousand copies. But 'Counting Stars' went on to become one of the biggest songs of that year so I guess at least we lost out to a good track. The fact we were even in the top ten with our first release was incredible to us, and it was such a relief we weren't a massive flop.

**TRISTAN:** We got busy really quickly after 'Can We Dance' charted, and the first big TV we ever did was *Big Brother's Bit on the Side*. We were petrified. There were potentially three or four million people watching the show. Nothing can prepare you for that.

**CON:** We also did *Blue Peter* quite early on and we were supposed to just stand and watch from the side until we were introduced. But Tristan walked right out onto the stage with the presenters. Because it was live, we were all standing there looking at him, thinking 'Noooooo!'

LIFE ON THE ROAD

MISSED FLIGHTS, MESSY
ROOMS AND BARBECUES
WITH SUPERSTARS

**CON:** It was slightly less nerve-wracking releasing our second single, 'Wild Heart', because we knew what to expect. It went in at number two and then dropped to number three by the Sunday, but all the singles from the first album went top ten, which is amazing. We were really pleased.

**BRAD:** You can never tell how a single will do and even now we get nervous when we release a new one. Everyone can tell you you've got a massive hit on your hands but then radio stations might not play it and it may not go as big as you hoped.

We shot the 'Wild Heart' video in the middle of the desert and it was freezing. You'd think it would be warm but it was so cold when we arrived at 6 a.m. I was wearing stripy socks and they wanted me to wear plain ones for the video, so I had to borrow a pair from this girl on set and they were all wet and sweaty.

**JAMES:** We supported The Wanted on tour the month after 'Wild Heart' came out, and that was really weird because it was their last-ever tour. The Wanted lads were all upset about it and we felt terrible for them. But we loved getting to hang out with the guys and travel around the country again. Travelling is one of the things we enjoy most.

**BRAD:** In the early days of the band, seven of us travelled around in this tiny little van. It was us and then Dean, our videographer, Fin, our tour manager, and Joe, our other manager. It was awesome fun. We'd have all our gear in the boot and there were six seats in the back and three in the front, so it brought everyone pretty close.

A lot of the fans knew what the van looked like so they'd often spot it when we were leaving gigs or interviews. One time we were leaving a venue in Manchester and the fans were already walking up the road. We got stuck in a traffic jam and someone spotted us. Within minutes everyone cottoned on to the fact that it was us and a few hundred people surrounded the car.

We couldn't move and some people were banging so hard on the windows we thought they were going to break. It was only us four, Fin and another tour manager called Davey, who was driving. Because we were pretty new then we didn't have any security with us or anything.

In the end Fin had no choice but to call the police. When they arrived they separated all the cars in front of us so we could drive through. That was one of our craziest experiences. I felt really bad for Davey. It was the first time he'd worked with us and he ended up in the middle of a police escort.

TRISTAN: We also had another scary moment in Manchester once. A fan caught up with us as we were driving really slowly down a side road and she pulled the handle of one of the back doors and opened it. It was one of those doors that slides to the side and Joe was sitting next to it and nearly fell out! We had to grab him to stop him falling into the road.

Another fan who had been running to catch up with us was so distracted by what happened she ran straight into a lamppost, but thankfully she was OK. All in all, it wasn't the greatest exit we've ever made.

JAMES: The fans are amazing at finding out where we are. Con and I were sharing a hotel room in Manchester once. We were opposite Tristan and Brad and the door was on the latch so we could go in and out of each other's room.

There was a knock on the door and we thought it was room service so we shouted, 'Come in.' Suddenly six girls we didn't know ran into our room! It felt quite intrusive in a way. They were really nice and they left when we asked them to, but it was quite scary.

TRISTAN: We lived in hotels together for about six months when the band first started, and it was different every time because we always used to swap around rooms. In the really early days (BC), James, Brad and I would share as a three-piece and it drove James mad. Brad and I are like crazy people when we're together so James is very relieved we get our own rooms now.

JAMES: We still share hotel rooms every now and again and because it's not that often I enjoy it. We have different habits in that I like going to bed early and the other guys like waking up late.

If you want to stay up late you share with Brad, and if you want to stay up and go out you stay with Con. If you don't want to sleep you share with Tris, and according to the boys if you want a political debate and healthiness you share with me.

Who we share with definitely has an effect on what we do. If Brad shares with me he's more likely to go to the gym, but if he shares with Con he could end up going to the gym *or* going out for a big one. It's a bit of a gamble.

CON: We do some really stupid things when we're travelling sometimes. Tris and I call ourselves 'The Project'. Once when we were in a hotel in LA we had a connecting room with Joe and Dean. We set an alarm at 4 a.m. and got up, put balaclavas on and went into their room with bottles of caesar salad dressing and some garlic butter. We tipped it all over their heads and it ended up on the lampshades and all up the wall. And while it was funny, it was also really annoying because we had to clean it up.

TRISTAN: Joe and Dean got their revenge by putting all of our boxer shorts into the safe and they refused to tell us the code.

They also put shaving foam inside all of our stuff. It was all pretty ridiculous but you've got to keep yourself amused, haven't you?

BRAD: Con and I once got a bit overexcited after a show and we threw two chocolate eclairs at the wall in our hotel room. Usually bands throw TVs, but we threw cakes. We felt really guilty after, and we had to pay for the damage to the wall. It was the least rock 'n' roll thing ever.

We tend to be with the same crew all the time when we're travelling – although it's obviously a bigger team if we're touring.

# JOE
## MANAGER. MUSICIAN. HAIR ICON.

**BRAD:** Joe has been there from day one and he's such a lovely guy. He helped to get the band together and he used to come along and write with us all in the very early days. We learnt a lot about hooks, melodies and the progression of a song from him.

He's seen us grow up and he's been so supportive throughout everything. He's always there to talk to and have a drink with. And he's very good at finding us cool places to go and explore on our days off.

# FIN
## TOUR MANAGER. ORGANISER. ROCK GOD.

**CON:** Fin was the bass player in a rock band called Hell is for Heroes, and he toured for about ten years, so he came fully loaded with loads of information to pass on. It was amazing going on our first tour with someone who could restring a guitar and set up a drum kit.

He's been with us right from the beginning and makes sure we're where we need to be, when we need to be there. We've probably been a nightmare at times but he lays the law down when he needs to. He's a bit of a touring father figure and a great person to look after us.

# DEAN
## VIDEOGRAPHER. DUDE. *FIFA* DEMON.

**TRISTAN:** As we've mentioned, Dean filmed our first-ever proper cover video for YouTube, and it was partly because of that we got signed. Dean even came down to my house while we were rehearsing for the McFly tour, and I think a lot of our success is down to the material he's captured.

He's very laidback and always calm in a crisis. We call the band and Fin, Dean and Joe 'The Tight Seven', because we're always together.

# RICHARD
## MANAGER. MUSIC GURU. LEGEND.

**JAMES:** Richard is the brains behind the operation and I don't think we could have asked for a better manager. He's always guided us and allowed us to be creative, while he sorts out the tricky side of things.

He loves music and loves seeing bands do well. He 100 per cent puts us first. He will go to war for us on anything and he'll always fight our corner. We owe so much to him.

**CON:** We've been to so many amazing places with the band already, and we've got more scheduled in. We feel incredibly lucky.

My favourite place to visit in the world is Australia. We went to a place called the Blue Mountains and it was the most amazing thing I've ever seen. There were waterfalls and beautiful scenery and we went on a hike for hours. I don't even like hiking that much but that was amazing. We got to chill out in the sun and go sailing on catamarans.

Florida was cool too, but we nearly ended up in trouble while we were out there. Tris, Brad and I were all in the sea on inflatable animals (mine was a crocodile, by the way). We linked them together in a triangle because we were talking and sunbathing, and when we looked up there was a guy swimming towards us really fast. He was waving his arms and shouting and we thought he was coming over to say hello. But it turned out it was a lifeguard who had come to tell us that the beach had been shut all day because of sharks. We'd drifted pretty far out and he saved us from getting eaten, which was very nice of him.

**JAMES:** Travelling is incredible but weirdly tiring. I love going to visit new places but we don't always get a lot of time to see the place properly. When we last went to Japan I went on a train to a temple that was an hour and a half away from where we were staying because I always try and maximise the time I have.

The first time we ever went to America as a band (this was BC, because Connor wasn't officially a Vamp then) was in January 2013 when we went to record some tracks for the first album.

We went to New York first and we stayed in an apartment, which is crazy looking back because we were only sixteen or seventeen. I'd never even been to New York and it was minus 12. When you're walking back from the studio at 3 a.m. that's pretty cold.

On our first day there we went to a supermarket to do some food shopping. I got some vegetables and chicken (it was before I was vegetarian) so I could make some healthy, balanced meals.

Brad got some burgers, pasta and sauces, and Tristan arrived at the checkout with a box of Lucky Charms, a pizza, some beef jerky, bacon and a packet of bubble gum. The only thing you could sort of call a meal was the pizza, and he burnt that when he tried to cook it.

**BRAD:** I was really intent on us all eating together and I was going to try and make us some pasta for dinner. Tristan and I ended up having an argument because he'd bought some bacon and I suggested that we use it in the pasta. He wasn't having any of it even though there were eighteen rashers in the packet and I got really angry with him. I think that was probably the first time we ever fell out.

Tristan and I were so messy. We were just kids and we were living on our own for the first time so we never, ever cleaned up. I'm not sure we knew how to. The apartment we were staying in was a total mess. There was mould in the bottom of cups and rotting food and it smelt really bad. We still had a great time though.

**JAMES:** By the end of the two weeks it was driving me a bit mad. I didn't even go to the gym back then so I had no way to escape from

them. That's the only time we've lived together and I would like to never do it again.

It's a shame Con wasn't there because he's probably the easiest to live with out of all of us. He's so easy and chilled out. He's really good at knowing when other people need space, but we weren't very good with that on that trip so we drove each other a bit mad.

Despite all the claustrophobia, that was my favourite America trip because even though the apartment was a state and we worked really hard, everything was so new and exciting. We were a bit scared to leave the apartment unless we were going to the studio because New York seemed so crazy, and of course none of us could drink so it wasn't like we could go to a bar. But I loved that time.

TRISTAN: We were working on the first album over there and we got put together with these producers called Espionage, who have worked with people like Beyoncé and Train. They're very cool and it was a big thing for us to be working with them when we were so new.

**BRAD:** They were an amazing team but we were pushing ourselves really hard and we were working until 2 a.m. or 3 a.m. every morning. I was singing for seven hours at a time, and the night before we were leaving New York I was so exhausted I walked out of the vocal booth and started crying.

It was my first time away for ages, I was feeling quite homesick, and my throat was really sore. James came and gave me a hug and we had a chat and I told him how exhausted I was feeling.

It did make me think, 'Is this what it's going to be like all the time?' I knew if I carried on with the same momentum I'd be really ill and it wasn't worth risking my voice.

That was the first time we realised how important it is to stay healthy and that you can't do too much at once. I learnt how to take care of my voice and how well I had to treat it, because it's not invincible.

In a strange way that whole episode made me stronger because I began to understand my voice more. And I also learnt how to say no when I have too much pressure put on me.

By the end of the two-week trip we got amazing vocals so the producers did get the best out of me, but I still don't think you should ever push a vocalist too much.

I went to see a doctor before we left New York and luckily I hadn't done any permanent damage to my throat, but my vocal folds were really inflamed which meant I was struggling to swallow.

I was feeling pretty low and when we got on the plane to fly to our next destination, Los Angeles, I had a massive panic attack. I don't like flying anyway and I felt like my throat was closing up and I got really overwhelmed with everything. Thankfully LA was just what we all needed.

**TRISTAN:** We went to LA to work with some other writers and it was sunny and relaxed. Our hotel had a Jacuzzi and Brad got a chance to recover.

We only got one song recorded, 'Love Struck', while we were out there so we had a lot of downtime. We went exploring on our skateboards and had so much fun. It didn't feel like work. We were just having a massive laugh.

**BRAD:** We stayed at the Hilton out by Universal City and we still try and stay there when we visit LA now. We met a waiter and it's always nice when you know people at hotels. It makes it feel more homely in a way.

We gave him a big tip on our last day and now whenever we eat in the restaurant he brings us out these massive sundaes even though we don't ask for them.

LA is somewhere we always enjoy going to. The Philippines is an amazing place to visit, too, and I don't think they get that many bands out there so they were so excited to see us.

The fans in Japan are so respectful. They always turn out for signings or appearances and they're really dedicated. They can be quite loud when we see them at airports and things, but when we play a gig they're so polite they even clap between songs. Sometimes it's so silent in the venues you can hear a pin drop. James and Con have spoken to each other across the stage at gigs before because it's so quiet.

We went to fashion designer Roberto Cavalli's outdoor club when we were in Milan once and that was so cool. It had this lift in the middle and you could go to the top of this tower and look out the city.

**CON:** It's mad that we've got fans all around the world. When we went to Manila there were 3,000 girls waiting for us in a shopping centre. Being able to sell out tours in Australia, Hong Kong and Singapore before we'd even been there was insane, but we're so grateful.

48

**TRISTAN:** Not everything has run smoothly when we've been travelling. I nearly missed a flight home from LA after my phone, passport and credit cards got nicked from a dressing room while we were performing.

I had to go to the British Embassy and get an emergency passport, but I left it under a pizza box on the tour bus and the driver threw it away by mistake. Joe and I had to go through all the bins but eventually Joe found it, thank God.

I managed to get back to the UK but we were due to fly to Sweden two days later and I couldn't fly on my temporary passport.

**BRAD:** We were going to support a band called The Fooo Conspiracy, who are massive in Sweden. We didn't think Tris would be able to come out so our drum tech, Ryan, flew back from a holiday with his wife specially to fill in.

In the end Tristan managed to get a passport and get the flight out on the day of the gig so we felt terrible for Ryan.

Tristan came on stage wearing a skeleton mask and sat behind his drum kit. Because we'd told the audience he wasn't coming he wanted to whip his mask off and do a big reveal a couple of songs in, but I totally forgot to introduce him.

**TRISTAN:** The audience just saw this absolute weirdo playing the drums in a *Scream* mask. I was waiting to take my mask off and surprise everyone but Brad didn't set it up. In the end I gave up and took the mask off anyway because I was sweating like mad. I waited for some kind of reaction and no one screamed. Literally, no one. I've never felt less cool in my life.

**CON:** Brad and I nearly missed an early morning flight to Bahrain a while back, but that was for very different reasons.

We went out with All Time Low and a band called The Tide for 'a couple of drinks' the night before and, funnily enough, that didn't work out very well. We got in at 5 a.m. and we had to be at the airport at 6 a.m.

Brad and I were living together in an apartment in London and our manager Joe had to break in to wake us up. I'd gone to sleep fully clothed and when I woke up I had no idea what was going on. I've never felt that bad in my life. I went to sleep on the flight but I woke up feeling just as rough the other end.

**BRAD:** That was so awful. We were supposed to be picking Tristan up forty-five minutes before we had woken up. I was totally naked and I ran into Con's room and he was face-down passed out on the bed so I slapped him really hard on the ass. We were running around trying to do ten things at once and it was a nightmare.

Con and I also missed a flight to Italy after a night out once, and everyone was very unimpressed. Poor Fin had to stay behind at the airport and wait for us and he still hasn't forgiven us.

I'm the one who's always late after a night out. But then, I'm always late full stop.

One time we were working out in Dubai and I ended up getting to bed at 6 a.m. because there was a club and karaoke room in the hotel. We were hanging out with Rita Ora, Young Jeezy, Trey Songz and – here's the killer – it was free booze. The problem with free drink is you just never know how much you're having because you don't have to go to the bar and physically hand over any money.

I set my alarm but it didn't go off (I swear I set it) and I woke up to find Fin standing over me looking really angry. That was the scariest moment of my life. I was nearly an hour late to meet everyone and we had to get a flight so it was a close call.

I looked so ill on the plane the flight the attendant asked me if I was going to be OK to fly. You know you're looking rough when that happens. I spent the whole time thinking I was going to throw up.

**JAMES:** That reminds me of the time when Tristan was ill and he was sitting next to me on a flight throwing up the entire time. It was a really cramped flight and all I could smell was Tristan's sick. He only gets migraines about once a year but when he does they disable him so I felt bad for him. But equally I really, really wanted him to stop.

I've only missed one flight, but that wasn't due to going out. We were due to do some Christmas gigs in America in 2015 so we were flying out in mid-December. We did a show in Liverpool and then we drove to Manchester and stayed in a hotel so we could get a really early flight the next morning.

I'm always the first to get on the plane because I like being prompt. As I went to board the plane the crew were randomly selecting people for additional security. They grabbed my bag and asked me to stand to one side. This guy walked off and when he came back ten minutes later he told me they'd found evidence of explosives on my bag.

We'd had pyros on the stage at the gig the night before and I'd got some of the residue on my hands. When I came off stage and put stuff in my bag I'd transferred it and it was still there the following day.

Security spent about an hour and a half taking everything out my backpack and swabbing all of my belongings individually. Pretty much all of my stuff came up as having explosive materials on them, and the upshot was that I wasn't allowed on the flight. We were due to perform in Baltimore so the other guys flew to New York and then got on a tour bus, but Joe and I had a nightmare 24-hour journey via Florida in the end.

I had to replace all of my gear at Florida airport and Joe offered to go off and buy me a new laptop case. When he came back he

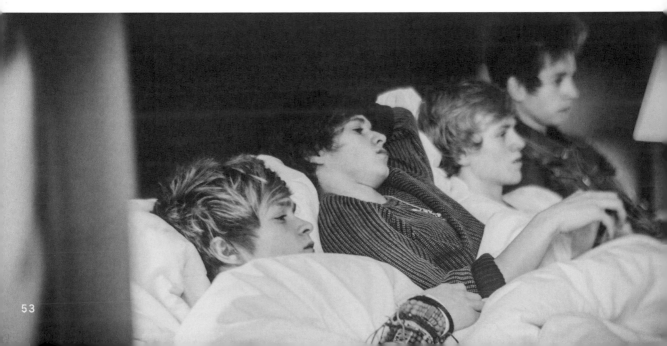

claimed the only one he could find was bright pink, so now I have to carry this fuchsia case around with me all the time. I'm sure he did it on purpose as punishment.

**CON:** I'm the one who sleeps most on planes, but being a good sleeper is both brilliant and bad.

We got invited to play the Capital Summertime Ball in front of 75,000 people at Wembley Stadium in 2013. It was the biggest show we'd ever done and we were really excited because it was an opportunity for us to really promote our music. Everyone arranged to meet in the lobby of our hotel in London but I didn't show up and no one knew where I was.

**TRISTAN:** We called his room and his phone but there was no answer, so we all went up to try and find him. We knocked on the door but there was no response and it took us about ten minutes for us to get a key so we were really panicking. We went in and he was fast asleep in bed. He's such a deep sleeper he sleeps through phone calls and alarms and all sorts. When he woke up he looked really confused and had no idea why we were there. Imagine if we'd missed that gig!

**CON:** It is bad. The other lads take videos of me sleeping on planes and put them on Instagram sometimes. I'm always worried about snoring because I got into such a deep sleep so quickly.

**JAMES:** We've got to hang out with some amazingly cool people when we've been abroad too.

When we were in LA filming our video for 'Wake Up' with Brooklyn Beckham, the Ramsay family came along to our gig and I got on really well with Jack. Gordon invited us for a barbecue the following day and it was us, the Ramsays, the Beckhams and James Corden.

I looked over at one point and David Beckham was in the pool chilling out and it's things like that which make me take a step back and take in what we're doing.

**TRISTAN:** It was such a nice vibe at the barbecue because all the kids were running around having fun and everyone was so down to earth. It was nice to see how 'normal' they are. We were all chatting to David and Victoria – they're such a great couple. Victoria is such an amazing businesswoman and she's done so well.

Brooklyn is so cool. He's a normal, nice, good-looking guy. He's got good genes! He's got a lot going on in his life and I think everyone assumed he would be a footballer, but he's really into photography and he's very creative. He's going to do something interesting with his life for sure.

**JAMES:** It is crazy working with people we admire so much.

We got invited over to Taylor Swift's house in Beverly Hills for dinner too. I'd been a fan for years so it was like a dream for me. I think she's one of the greatest role models the world can have.

**CON:** Her house was lovely and really darkly lit and cosy. It was so nicely furnished and she's got a grand piano in one of her rooms. She was so friendly and down to earth and she made us feel really comfortable.

I was slightly mortified because she made a massive curry but I've got a nut allergy so I couldn't eat it. I made Joe tell her because I was too scared. She was really sweet and made me some plain brown rice to eat instead.

I felt terrible when she'd made such an effort to look after us. But it would have been much more embarrassing if I'd ended up being rushed to hospital after eating her food.

BRAD

# 'JAMES SPOTTED ME ON YOUTUBE AND CONTACTED ME VIA FACEBOOK, THE MASSIVE STALKER.'

When James first sent me a message on Facebook I nearly didn't reply to him. I thought it was a bit weird that some guy I'd never met was contacting me out of the blue. He could have been anyone.

It's crazy to think about what would have happened if I hadn't ever messaged him back. My life would be so different right now.

I was born and raised in Sutton Coldfield in the West Midlands and I've lived in the house that's still our family home since I was two. I've got one older sister called Natalie who is twenty-five and is a qualified barrister. She went to uni in Bristol and she ended up staying there, and it's weird not having her around.

I miss her and sometimes it feels like I'm an only child. We got on really well the whole time we were growing up (well, most of the time), which is really unusual. We had the odd spat but nothing big.

I've always been very family orientated and it's really just the four of us. I was really close to my nan on my mum's side, but she died about a year ago. She had a great life though and was an amazing woman. She was a contortionist in the circus and she's the only other entertainer in our family. I certainly didn't inherit her bendiness.

I was also close to my mum's brother and my grandad on my dad's side. Unfortunately they have passed away in the past couple of years, but were both great men.

I trust my family more than anyone else in the world and I know they'll be there for me throughout everything. We're a really tight group.

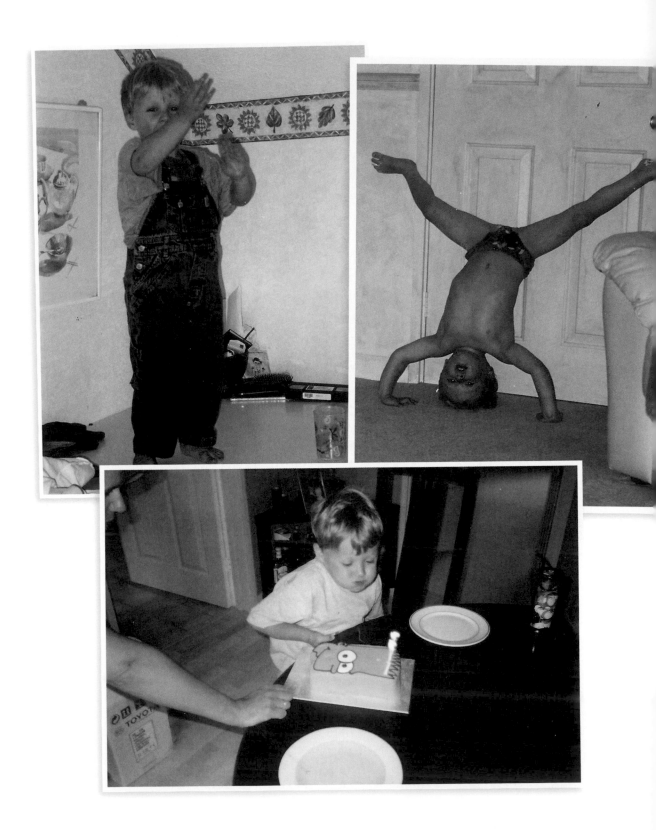

People are often surprised that I still live at home with my mum and dad, but I am so close with them. My mum has been my rock from day one. She's supported me no matter what and is my moral compass, and I'm eternally grateful for having such an amazing mother – fanks mum! My dad has always been a joker and sometimes I want to slap him in the face, but he always manages to make me look on the bright side and make me laugh.

I do think about moving to London every so often but I can walk around Sutton and say hello to about twelve people in an hour, but London is so anonymous I could walk around there for a year and not know anyone. I would like to move to London for a year or two at some point but I would have to live with a mate from home or someone I really trusted so I had proper grounding.

I wasn't the big personality who always wanted attention at school. I enjoyed sport and hanging out with my mates more than anything. I wasn't shy, but I wasn't the most outgoing kid in my class.

I'm clearly terrible with timekeeping, and I was bad even as a kid. I got about ninety-nine lates one term so I'd get loads of detentions.

I also hated wearing my school uniform, especially the trousers. I'm not saying I wanted to wear a skirt or anything, honest, but I didn't see why we couldn't wear skinny jeans instead. It really annoyed me.

I've worn bracelets all my life and we weren't allowed those either, and one day my PE teacher told me I had to cut them off so I wrapped duct tape around them in protest instead. I know, I was quite the rebel.

I got into music when I was around ten, and at that time I'd listen to whatever my mum played, which could have been anything from AC/DC and Led Zeppelin to Jamiroquai and Stevie Wonder.

Jamiroquai was actually the first concert I ever went to when I was about seven and I hated it because it was so loud. I had really bad problems with my ears when I was younger. I used to get ear infections and I had to have grommets, as well as two operations on each ear. I was never allowed to take part in swimming classes at school because it was painful to go underwater, and my poor mum was always having to take me to the doctor.

I still have to get my ears checked every so often now, and I did wonder if being in the band would affect my hearing. Luckily, I haven't had a problem so far, so fingers crossed that continues.

My ear problems were so bad they caused me to have a speech impediment growing up. I used to hear 'ch' as a 'sh' sound, so that's how I pronounced them. I spoke like that until I was seventeen and it was only singing and teaching myself to say 'ch' at front of my mouth instead of the back that kind of cured it. I was pleased but my mum was a bit gutted because she thought the way I spoke was really cute.

I had a lot of mates at primary school but I went to a different secondary school to everyone else so I didn't know *anyone* when I arrived on my first day. I did end up meeting new friends pretty quickly, like Jack, Mike, and the two Alexs who I'm still close to now.

I really liked PE at primary school, and then at secondary school geography became my favourite subject. I could have totally imagined myself studying geography at uni. I also liked business studies but I hated maths because I was terrible at it. I think there are two different types of people: those who are good at English and those who are good at maths (which is my excuse for being rubbish at maths). I'm definitely in the English category because I liked the creativity of it.

Secondary school was when I first got seriously interested in music, and that's also when I started playing guitar. I had lessons with a guy called Carl Archer for about two years, and he taught me a lot about improvising rather than classic conventional guitar teaching.

I was in a band called Relentless. One of my best mates Josh was the drummer, a guy called Sam was on bass, one of my best mates Jack was a guitar player and my mate Luke was the singer. Jack and I started writing songs together and we all used to practise in the music cupboard whenever we had time. Then Luke left the band because of musical differences (it was a big deal at the time) and eventually we broke up.

I started doing solo acoustic music for a while, and then Sam and I teamed up and formed a duo called Einstein and Eddington, which I

still think is a great name. I was also in a band called The Cardboard Cutouts and The Spectrum Effect. I don't care what anyone says, all of those names were winners.

The first album I ever bought was by a band called Wheatus, and shortly afterwards I bought The Fratellis' *Costello Music* and *Monster* by The Automatic from a garage sale down my road. I was big into indie music like Bloc Party and The Pigeon Detectives.

The other thing I was into in my teens was skateboarding. It was one of those things I loved as soon as I tried it. My mate James and I used to jump on the bus and go to a youth centre called Clifton in Sutton all the time. They had a big concrete basketball court and every Thursday they'd put in ramps and transform it into a skate park.

I ended up getting quite good because I'm small so I've got a lower centre of gravity. The youth centre used to run skateboarding tournaments and I came top in my category. I won a skateboard and I was so pleased, but I managed to snap it within three days.

As well as skating I played football for my local team, and I still love football now. All in all I was a pretty active teenager, which is funny considering I'm so lazy now. I was a fourteen-year-old, long-haired, sweaty mess, but skateboarding gave me a bit of kudos. I hope.

That was around the time I met my first-ever girlfriend. We were together from when we were fourteen and we were childhood sweethearts. Even now I compare other relationships to that one. We grew up together and I trusted her completely, and your first love is always a really important one. We're still friends now and we keep in touch.

My mum and sister were big fans of *Desperate Housewives* when I was growing up so my first celebrity crush was Eva Longoria. I also liked Eva Mendes and Zooey Deschanel because she's so funny.

I was pretty well behaved at school but I had a couple of naughty mates so I sometimes got into trouble by association. It was mainly due to lack of concentration and laziness. My school reports often said, 'Brad has a lot of potential but he doesn't apply himself.' One of my teachers told my parents he wanted to put a rocket under my chair, which says it all.

The problem with me is that I only like doing stuff that interests me. That's why I worked hard at music – because I had a real passion for it. But any subjects I didn't like I pretty much ignored.

I went back to my school for a Sport Relief fundraiser a while ago and my head of sixth form was there. He still took the mickey out of my hair like he always used to, and I went straight back to being a seventeen-year-old boy again.

I used to do a lot of music stuff down in Cornwall because we went there every Easter for a family holiday. I wrote my first song there when I was thirteen. It was called 'My Window', and it was about moving to Cornwall. It boasted the lyric: 'Cornwall's outside my window'. Poignant.

I was constantly writing songs and I still write all the time now because I feel weird if I don't. I never think, 'I should write a song today.' It's more like: 'I *need* to write a song today.' Some people punch a boxing bag or go for a run if they're feeling stressed, but I write music. I feel like I've got something out my system afterwards.

One day when I was fifteen I decided to try busking in Cornwall. I wanted to try and sell some CDs too so I recorded some songs on my Mac – four original tracks and some covers of bands like Oasis – and then I watched a video on YouTube about how to make a CD cover. I got ten pieces of cardboard, drew a landscape of a city on each of them and wrote 'Bradley Will Simpson' in big letters underneath.

I made about £40 from busking, and the same night I went to an open mic night in a pub near where we were staying. It was pretty packed with tourists and I sang a mash-up of Wild Cherry's 'Play That Funky Music' and Stevie Wonder's 'Superstitious'. I sold all ten of my CDs and pocketed another £40. Buzzing!

Music has been at the forefront of everything for me for years now. I'm not sure when music became the most important thing in my life, but there came a point where I loved singing and performing more than anything else. I entered a talent show at school singing a song I'd written called 'Boom Boom Kapow'. It was about being a superhero and a couple of my mates still sing it to me now because they think it's hilarious.

I wasn't one of those people who tried out for all the school plays because I wasn't brave enough. I've become more confident now and I really like doing little bits of acting when we get the opportunity, but back then the biggest thing I did was take part in our end-of-year show singing Take That's 'Never Forget'.

I started gigging on my own when I was sixteen. I met a promoter and he started to get me gigs in Birmingham. He worked with a lot of up-and-coming artists so I'd support them and sell my EPs at the same time.

I got my EP done after my parents bought me a studio session as a present. I went along and recorded five songs, and my sister took some photos for the CD cover. My dad's friend had a printing company so he printed them up for me, and I used to take them around with me and hope people would fork out for them.

I gigged a lot and it was an amazing way to get experience, but because I'm so lazy I used to get booked for gigs and then when it came to the night I didn't want to go. It was so out of order and thankfully my mum used to make me go to *most* of them.

I was getting really good feedback from people (when I did turn up) and that's when I started feeling brave enough to put covers up on YouTube. I chose songs by bands I was into like Two Door Cinema Club and The Arctic Monkeys, and I also did a cover of Ed Sheeran's 'Lego House'. It was probably the worst cover I've ever done but somehow it got traction and ended up with about 60,000 views.

I didn't see music as a full-on career as much as something I could *do*. It was something I enjoyed so I guess I almost took it for granted.

I never thought I was amazing at it or I was going to be a big singer, partly because I didn't have the get up and go for it back then. I was generally more interested in playing *FIFA* or watching TV because that required little effort.

I never consciously did anything to become famous. When the first series of *The Voice* started I did think about going on that, but in the end I backed out. The only time I really made a go of things was when Jamie Cullum ran a competition in collaboration with Pizza

Express, because he got discovered in one of their restaurants. The top ten people who got through got to meet Jamie and potentially get a record deal, and the song I performed for the competition is still up on YouTube. Sadly I didn't get through to the final but I did see Jamie Cullum at an airport once. That's pretty much the same thing, isn't it? Not *really*?

It was thanks to my YouTube videos that James spotted me and messaged me via Facebook, the massive stalker. As I mentioned before, I didn't reply for ages because I didn't know who he was and it all seemed a bit off. But then I decided I had nothing to lose.

I was really nervous because I'd never been approached by anyone about my music before and I didn't know how it all worked. I was also sceptical about whether the manager James was working with, Richard, was really who he said he was. James told me that Richard had managed Busted and McFly before, and it all seemed too good to be true. James had more of an idea about how the music business ran and I was clueless, so I trusted his judgement.

James had met loads of different musicians before he contacted me but we clicked straight away. He's very laidback like I am and we both knew we wanted to be in a band and make music, so we had the same goals too. He ended up coming to stay with me one weekend so we could try playing music together and we got on so well. God, it sounds like a first date!

James became the first person I properly wrote songs with. We'd get little videos together and send them to Richard and he'd give us feedback, and we'd go back and play around with them until we got them right.

The first time I met Richard was at a hotel in London. I went along with my parents and I found it all quite strange because I knew that this meeting could turn my life on its head.

Joe, our other manager, turned up with a guitar on his back. He looked like he could be a member of the band and we hit it off straight away.

I played Richard and Joe a couple of songs, including 'Boom Boom Kapow'. I was quite intimidated but they were really complimentary and said they liked my voice and songwriting. What a relief.

That was my first interaction with a music manager and I've met a lot since who are nothing like them. Some managers will use people for what they can get or they're untrustworthy.

Our tour manager, Fin, was in a big band for years and they went through seven managers in their career, but we hit the jackpot straight away. Richard is such an intelligent man and he's so talented. He doesn't do his job for the money; he does it purely because he wants to see a band succeed, and that's such a rarity. He's not jaded at all and he still finds it all exciting. The first thing he always asks us is if we've had enough rest, and he never pushes us to do things we don't want to.

The name The Vamps came about six months into me and James working together. We were going through names with Richard and he suggested it. We hated it at first but we ended up going with it. We put a cover out under that name and it stuck. Now it feels right and I think it suits us and it sticks in people's minds. I guess if someone had suggested the name Arctic Monkeys to us and they weren't already a famous band we'd have thought that was completely ridiculous, but it really suits them.

And then came Tristan. He'd heard about James through a friend and contacted him on Facebook (there's a pattern here). The three of us messaged each other and talked about music for ages, and then we arranged to go to James's parents' house for the weekend to figure out if Tris could work in the band.

I first met him on a train because I hopped into his carriage four stops before Bournemouth. He was wearing red jeans and a blazer, which is basically his personality in clothing form. He used to love his coloured jeans. I was wearing a shirt buttoned right up to the top and a jumper so I looked really smart, and he still takes the mickey out of me for it.

James picked Tristan and me up from the station in his gold car (playa) and we immediately started messing around and recording videos. We took some of our recording equipment to James's house. We set two cameras up and felt well professional. The first cover we ever did was of a Lawson song, 'When She Was Mine', but that never saw the light of day.

After that we met up every weekend at one of our houses and then we started going to record labels. I was studying business, PE and geography at sixth form by that point, but my mind was totally on the music.

Tris came to Cornwall on our family holiday for a week a few months later and my parents loved it. We recorded some funny videos and it was wicked fun. All those little things helped us to bond and we were lucky that we had a really good chunk of time to get to know each other before we properly released anything. I think you need to go into this business being really solid because it's harder to form those friendships later on down the line.

Connor joined the band a little while later, and you've read how that came about. The first time I met Con he seemed really cool, but he was *so* shy. He's so different now. He's become much more comfortable with himself and he's really come out of his shell. He's a lovely lad.

I didn't really know what to expect from being in a band because I grew up reading *Kerrang!* and listening to rock bands. But because of the type of band we are, our image and personality are almost as important as the music, and that shocked me a bit. You never expect to get well known off the back of how you look or who you're dating, but that is all a part of it.

The press have been really good to us, and I think because we don't do things that are out of character we don't get negative things written about us. A newspaper once claimed we spent £10,000 in a nightclub, which we definitely didn't. I also got named as top clubber in the *Daily Mail* and I think I'd been out once that month, which was quite funny.

Because I read *Kerrang!* I thought interviews would be all about the music, but of course people want to know other things about us too. It can be a strange world and I've seen first hand how interested people can be in your private life. I'm not the biggest tweeter or Instagrammer in the world, and I'm open about the fact I find it quite difficult that people want to know everything about me.

I'm still not sure I'm used to it, but I am getting my head around it more. We owe everything to the fans and we know it's them who got us to where we are now. So I do want to share a lot, but I think I'm still getting to grips with how it all works.

I had a girlfriend who was also in a band called Fifth Harmony, and that was tricky. A lot was written about us after we split that wasn't true.

We met when we were both support acts for Austin Mahone in the US in July 2014, along with Shawn Mendes. It was our first American tour and after a couple of days Lauren and I got chatting and we started spending more time together. When the tour came to an end we stayed in touch and we started seeing each other.

We ended up going out together for about six months and it just so happened our schedules crossed over quite a lot. We were in LA at the same time, and then she came over to the UK when I had some time off so we got to hang out then.

She's big into her music and we like the same kind of artists and that's what we connected over. We also had shared experiences with both of us being in bands so we could talk to each other about anything.

Lauren is a really sweet, lovely girl and we had a great time, but by the following Christmas things got difficult because both of our bands were getting busier and we just didn't have time to see each other. We agreed it would be best if we left things because it was impossible to keep the relationship going, and we certainly didn't split on bad terms. We still chat every so often now and she's a genuinely nice girl.

Shortly after we broke up we did a series of interviews and I was constantly asked about my relationship with Lauren. Whenever one of us in the band gets asked a difficult question the other boys will step in and try to deflect it.

One time we were doing an interview with a radio station. It was about the fiftieth time I'd been asked whether or not I'd been dating Lauren so the lads tried to make a joke out of it to get me out of having to answer.

James said: 'I haven't dated her for a while,' then Tristan added: 'I was April to December.' James then said: 'We've all had a bit of a go,' and that comment kicked off a big social media storm.

James really didn't mean anything by it at all, it was literally just a joke which sounded bad out loud, but wasn't meant that way. But the interview got cut in such a way that the joke fell completely flat and it was completely misinterpreted. Just to make it worse they also cut out the part where we said what lovely girls Fifth Harmony are. What James said got taken totally out of context. He certainly never meant to offend anyone. It looked like we were being rude about Lauren, which is something we would *never* do.

Both our fans and Fifth Harmony's were at loggerheads on social media and a massive deal was made out of something that was a jokey off-the-cuff comment, not meant with any malice. I spoke to Lauren that day and she was totally fine about it and we cleared it all up, but other people wouldn't let it lie. The whole thing was horrible.

It's hard enough breaking up with someone as it is, so when this happened two months after the split it brought everything back to the surface and made things even harder.

I try not to be bothered about the things people say to me on social media but it's not always easy. If someone writes something negative about our music or something it's not so bad, but if it's personal that can really hurt. And a *lot* was written about that incident.

That was the only time I've been out with someone in the public eye and maybe I was naive about it. I guess in some ways it makes it easier if you go out with someone who is in the same business as you because you can trust each other. If you're on a similar level you know that person is unlikely to have an agenda and they're not looking to further themselves through you. But equally, if you're both stupidly busy, it makes it very hard to keep things going.

I'm more cautious when it comes to meeting girls now but I wish I didn't have to be. I've always been a really trusting person and now I'm just a bit more *aware*. I'm single at the moment and I'm fine with that because I would rather wait until I know someone is right. I'm determined to keep an open mind and take people at face value. It's easy to judge people too quickly and you could be missing out on someone great if you don't give them a chance.

Overall, being in the band is the best thing ever, and that's down to our fans. I always try my best to talk to them and hang out with them, and even if I'm in a bad mood I'll pull myself out of it and crack on. I think as soon as you stop doing that, you lose a sense of who you are. If you're not treating the people who have made you a success with respect there's something very wrong.

I have been called out on Twitter if I've been tired and I'm not bouncing around and being cheerful when I've met a fan, but sometimes we won't have had a lot of sleep and we have to go straight to work. There are times when we're a bit shattered so we may not be on top form.

But overall, being in The Vamps is ridiculously good. Some of the venues we've played in and the places we've visited are incredible. I love being in the studio too, because we get to indulge in our favourite hobby. It doesn't often feel like a job. It's just what we love doing and we get paid for it so it's wicked!

Headlining the O2 on our first proper tour was unbelievable. We were so excited when it sold out twice. That's 36,000 tickets! We were buzzing because we knew we were going to get to play to a sold-out O2 arena, and that was one of our dreams when we first started the band.

One of the best gigs we've ever played was at the Invictus Games, which Prince Harry is really involved in. The Foo Fighters are one of my favourite bands and they were headlining. The crowd were a lot older than our usual type of fans, and we basically played to thousands of burly men who didn't have a clue who we were. But I loved that gig because it was a bit of a challenge. I knew I had to try and get them on our side and I love that.

I almost prefer the gigs that are challenges sometimes, but equally I love performing for our fans because the atmosphere is always incredible and we love seeing them sing along to our songs.

Some of my other highlights in the band so far have been the two American tours we've done. When we tour in the UK we can generally be home in about three hours, unless we're in Ireland or Scotland. But in America you're on a bus for six weeks non-stop and it feels like proper touring. It's so cool.

When we did our first American tour our bus broke down after a week. There was another big tour going on so we couldn't get another bus, which meant we had to fly everywhere for five weeks. It was so tiring. It probably sounds glamorous, but it was one of the hardest things we've ever done and all of us were so run down.

It was brutal, but it taught us a lot and after that any other tour feels pretty easy-going. We had an amazing bus for the next American tour and it was such a wicked way to see the country. We'd come off stage, sit in the lounge and have beers, go to sleep and wake up in the next state. I really want to do that again one day. We all properly loved it.

I'll also always have great memories of the band's early days when we were constantly round each other's houses creating music. Richard used to say to us: 'This is going to be the most fun you'll have in the band, so cherish it.' And we used to think, 'Yeah, yeah, we just want to get out there and kick it all off.' But he was right to a certain extent.

There was no stress or pressure and we weren't in the limelight, so we were just a group of lads doing what we loved and getting to know each other. Those times will always feel special.

CONNOR

# 'I ONCE GOT LOCKED IN A TOILET IN MCDONALD'S.'

I'm definitely the most accident-prone member of The Vamps. Not only did I fall right off the end of a stage in front of around 20,000 people at the O2 in 2014 (not my finest moment), but thanks to a knee injury I spent a lot of early 2016 wearing a massive black leg brace.

But I'm getting way ahead of myself. You probably want to know a bit about my childhood before I start telling you about my various injuries/hospital visits?

I was born in Aberdeen in Scotland but my family moved to Warwick when I was four, so I spent the rest of my childhood around there. My dad is a pilot and my mum works for Estée Lauder, and I've got a younger brother called Louis who's thirteen and *massive*. He's six foot tall already. How unfair is that? My dad is also tall and I clearly got the short genes because I'm only five foot seven.

I was really happy when Louis came along because I'd always wanted a sibling, and we get on really well now. He's not fussed about me being in a band at all. He's really chilled out about it and all he wants to do when I go home is play PlayStation.

I was a pretty shy kid and quite chilled. I'm cool with being in my own company. My first memory is from right back when I was two years old and still living in Scotland. I remember having photos taken with my grandma by a bookshelf, and for some reason that's still really vivid and clear to me.

We lived with my grandparents for a while when we were in between houses and I remember a lot from about that time.

I spent the first year of reception at Balsall Common Primary School, and then we moved house and I went to a tiny school called Ferncumbe. There were only ten people in my class and it was nice

because everyone got on really well. It did mean I couldn't get away with anything though, because the teachers could keep an eye on us at all times. But to be fair, I don't think I would have been a particularly wild kid anyway.

I was pretty well behaved at school overall. I wasn't a goodie-goodie but I was quiet and I didn't get into trouble with the teachers. I was never going to be the lad at the back of the class shouting things or getting chucked out.

The only time I got into proper trouble was when I was fifteen and I got a talking-to from the police because my mates – not me! Promise – decided to throw rocks at a group of lads. We ran away and they chased us for a while and then, for some reason, they decided to phone the police instead, which to be honest was a massive relief. They were a lot older than us so they could have done us some serious damage.

I'd pulled a hamstring in my leg at the time (did I mention I'm accident prone?) so I would have been the first one they caught up with. My football career would have been over before it started. (Actually it never did start. But, you know ...).

I loved playing football so, needless to say, I also really liked PE at school because it meant we could play it during school time. I played four times a week out of school too, and for a time I was really set on becoming a professional player. I also liked learning Spanish so I chose to study it at high school. I can't speak it very well now but I can remember bits and pieces. When we're on nights out in Spanish-speaking countries I seem to think I'm fluent and start talking to people in what I think is perfect Spanish. I can order food when I go to Spain, which is the most important thing, right?

I liked listening to music when I was a kid but football was definitely my priority. Then, when I was twelve, my grandma gave me a guitar for Christmas. This is the point where I should pretend that I picked it up and instantly sounded like Ray Toro from My Chemical Romance, but no. Instead it sat around in my room for about a year gathering dust, and occasionally I'd throw clothes over it if I was too lazy to hang them up. Which, to be honest, was most of the time.

Then, one day, I picked the guitar up and started playing it and discovered I really enjoyed it. I just played for fun and at that point I definitely didn't think I could end up doing it long term. I didn't sing or anything so I just used to strum songs I liked and hope for the best.

I played guitar more and more, and eventually I gave up football and it became my main focus. I had a few lessons to start off with but then I taught myself most of it. I was into bands like Panic! at the Disco and All Time Low at the time, so I learnt some of their songs. And if I ever heard a track I liked on the radio or on YouTube I'd give that a go too.

The first album I ever bought was Busted's *A Present for Everyone*, and McFly and Busted were kind of the doorway into what I'm doing now. But I must admit I was pretty into S Club 7 too. I got their album for Christmas when I was eight so my excuse is that I was young and innocent and I didn't know any better.

My parents are into music and they like bands like The Stereophonics and Coldplay, so I listened to those kinds of groups growing up as well. I guess overall my early listening was quite mixed, but I always liked rockier music. S Club 7 was just a blip.

I started singing when I was about fourteen, but I wasn't very confident about it so it took me a while to sing in front of other people. It was only when I started a band with some mates from my music class at school that I came out of my shell a bit.

We called the band Sunset Skyline after we did a Facebook poll to find a name, and we took it really seriously. We used to talk about what we'd do when we became famous and we used to practise constantly. I don't think we were giving McFly sleepless nights or anything, but the other lads were really talented, and I think we were pretty good for our age.

Even though we tried really hard to get our foot in the door and get a manager, we didn't have any luck. We connected with one guy via YouTube, but nothing came of it and we all felt a bit frustrated. We were together for a couple of years in total and we kept the band going but it kind of took a backseat for me for a little while.

90

I'd been working on some solo stuff at home so I started uploading some acoustic covers to YouTube when I was about fifteen. I still wasn't feeling that confident, so I used a secret name on all my early videos. That way I could see if they got any views without anyone knowing it was me. If I got one bad comment I would delete the videos straight away, which is ridiculous because everyone gets some bad comments online, no matter who they are.

I was worried about people at school finding out I was singing in case they thought I was terrible, so I kept it under wraps for ages, and I didn't even tell my mates what I was doing. I was doing it more for myself in the beginning really, and I was trying to get better by making the videos and hopefully improving each time.

Eventually, once I was feeling a bit braver, I started playing some of the songs to my friends to get feedback. People were really positive and I also started to believe in what I was doing more as the months went on. I got to the point where I stopped worrying as much and I started recording more popular mainstream songs like tracks by Alex Clare, and I started putting my real name to them. I figured I had nothing to lose and that if I did get a negative comment it wasn't the end of the world.

I had two main groups of mates at school: my football mates and my music mates. I've known my football mates from when I was about six and we're still friends now. I'm also still really good friends with the guys from Sunset Skyline. I didn't really speak to them for a while after I left but it's great now. I've been producing some of the music they're doing with their new bands, which is another huge interest of mine.

My first big crush when I was a teenager was on Mila Kunis. I don't know many guys who don't like her to be fair. I also liked Anna Kendrick, Hayley Williams from Paramore and a girl called Tay Jardine from a band called We Are the In Crowd.

I started seeing my first girlfriend when I was fourteen and we were together for a long time, but we ended up splitting up after I joined The Vamps. Things went crazy and I was away so much we had to try and maintain our relationship via phone calls and Skype. We were used to spending so much time together and it made things really

hard. She wanted to be able to see someone every day, which is fair enough. In the end it got to the point where it was too difficult to keep the relationship going, so sadly we split up.

One of my best memories of school is of our prom. My mates and I hired a party bus thinking we were much older than we were. There was a massive party in the middle of a field afterwards. I have no idea who organised it but there was a bouncy castle and loads of people were really drunk.

One of my mates had a few too many, stole a pair of sunglasses from a garage and then ran down a motorway because he was scared he was going to get arrested. I think he was more likely to get arrested for running down a motorway than stealing the sunglasses ...

I did pretty well in my GCSEs and ended up with eight Bs, one C, one A and an A* in music. My original plan when I left school was to become an engineer because it felt like a 'safe' thing to do. I loved music but it still felt like trying to do it as a career was a huge gamble that might not pay off and I needed some kind of back-up. I was good at maths and physics so I went on to do them at A level, along with psychology, but it soon became clear I'd made the wrong choice. I didn't end up enjoying any of the subjects I'd chosen and I knew that if I carried on with the course I could end up wasting two years of my life. I knew music was what I really wanted to do, and if I didn't try and make a go of it, I would always be left wondering. I had nothing to lose at that age.

My parents were really understanding about me dropping out of sixth form, and I was lucky enough to get a place on a course studying music tech in Leamington Spa. But that ended up being pretty short-lived as well, because I ended up dropping out of there after six weeks when I joined the band!

I was introduced to The Vamps after a guy called Matt Martin spotted some of my videos online. He knows our manager Richard, and Richard had mentioned that he was looking for a bass player to join a band he was working with.

When I first spoke to Richard I must admit I was pretty sceptical. He told me he'd managed McFly and Busted and I thought, 'If that's true, that's awesome. And if it's not, this is all very strange.'

He filled me in on The Vamps, and funnily enough I knew who they were because I'd seen their acoustic covers on YouTube. That's when I realised Richard was for real and I arranged to go down to London to meet everyone.

I was only sixteen at the time so I was really nervous, but as soon as I met Brad, Tristan and James I knew I wanted to join the band. It was such a brilliant opportunity and they were such nice lads.

It was hard to form a proper impression of the guys from that first meeting because I was trying so hard to impress and I didn't really take everything in. But I remember thinking Tristan was a bit crazy ... And I was right.

I left the meeting feeling pretty optimistic but also incredibly nervous because I wanted it so badly. I knew I was going to be so gutted if it didn't work out.

Richard got in touch the following day and said the band were 'considering all their options'. The longer it all went on, the more desperately I wanted to be the fourth Vamp.

I continued doing more YouTube covers to keep the momentum going, and when James tweeted one of them I got some really positive feedback from their fans. I really hoped that would help to push things in the right direction.

Richard eventually got in contact with me two months – *two months!* – later, in December 2012. He told me I was still top of their list, and asked if I could go to Tristan's parents' house over New Year to hang out with the rest of the guys. Of course I said yes straight away.

We played games as an icebreaker, and it was a chance for us to have a laugh and get to know each other. The lads and I recorded some covers and we even filmed a video where we said: 'Hi, we're The Vamps.' I was like, 'Guys, should I be saying this too, or ... ?'

Tris, Brad and James put a video up on YouTube where they introduced me as 'our friend Connor, who is filling in on bass', which was another clever way of them trying me out to see if the fans liked me.

It was all looking really good and surely the fact that we'd hung out, got on really well and recorded some tracks together meant I was in? *Surely?*

But then I didn't hear anything.

I'll fast forward a bit, but the upshot is that after a bit more waiting (and then a bit more) they told me they didn't want me in the band (OK, clearly that didn't happen).

The first big thing we did as a band was go on tour with McFly as their support act. No pressure then.

Because I'm shy it was quite hard to be with a group of guys who had been hanging out with each other for the past year and knew each other really well, when I'd only met them properly a few times.

Thankfully they never made me feel like I was the odd one out. I was accepted straight away and we fell into being a four-piece really quickly. I think the tour helped massively because we were together constantly every single day and it was the perfect way to fast-track our friendships.

Tristan and I really bonded when I ended up in hospital in Manchester one night about halfway through the McFly tour.

I'd had some trouble breathing for a few days before, and then all of a sudden one day I was really struggling to catch my breath. My throat felt like it had closed up and everyone was really worried so I went to hospital to get checked out.

Tris and our tour manager Fin came with me and we had these really deep (and often quite odd) conversations while I was lying on a hospital bed. They were both great hospital companions and talking to them took my mind off everything.

At first, the doctors thought I had a heart condition, which didn't do anything to help my stress levels, but Tris and Fin helped me to stay calm. The hospital did a load of blood tests and monitored my heart, and all I could think about was how much I didn't want to miss the tour.

I ended up going back home to Warwick the following day and I went to another hospital for some more tests. I missed the gig in Cambridge that night, which I was gutted about, but thankfully I was soon given the all-clear so I was able to rejoin the tour pretty quickly.

It turned out I'd had a panic attack, which I think was caused by a combination of anxiety about being away from home and putting a lot of pressure on myself to do my absolute best each night. Once I knew what it was I able to deal with it more easily and stop panicking about panicking, if you know what I mean.

Danny from McFly was really supportive and he gave me good advice. In fact, the whole band did, and we ended up becoming mates with them, which seemed so crazy. They'd inspired us all to get into music and now we were hanging out with them. How does that even happen?

My anxiety carried on for a few months afterwards and sadly there wasn't a lot I could do about it except keep reminding myself that I was going to be OK. I had to learn to relax and not stress myself out (not always easy when you're performing for thousands of people each night) and just work through it. The more I got used to being on stage and travelling, the less I noticed it happening, and the other guys were a huge support.

Aside from the whole anxiety nightmare, being on tour was a really exciting time because we were staying in hotels and visiting great cities all the time. I hadn't travelled much at that point so I loved seeing new places.

Being from Scotland I loved going to Glasgow. Most of my family are still up there so they came to see the show and it felt amazing knowing there were so many people I knew in the audience. It made me feel properly proud.

Back then we didn't have a crew or security or anything so we were setting up all our equipment for the shows each night ourselves, and then taking it back down at the end of the night. We used to have a nightly competition to see how fast we could dismantle our gear. I'm sure Fin only did it because he wanted to get out of the venues as quickly as possible. He used to have a stopwatch and time us and everything. We got it down to ten minutes in the end, which we were very pleased with.

Those early days were insane now I look back on them. One day I was living with my parents and being looked after, and then next I was touring with a band and I had to become pretty self-sufficient. I'd never been away from home for that amount of time before. But then, neither had the other guys. It was like we were a family all learning at the same time. Because Fin was in a band himself for years he knew how it all worked so he showed us the ropes, and we all mucked in and got the hang of it in no time. We're still learning new things every day now, which keeps things exciting.

I had to grow up pretty fast in the band because even things like buying my own food were totally new to me. My mum always used to cook for me and I went straight from having my dinner made each night to buying fast food in service stations and getting room service every night.

I ate so many chips on that tour James banned me from eating any more. He's so healthy and he was horrified by how much beige food I ate. I am trying to be healthier though, and James is starting to influence me.

James and I are on totally different ends of the spectrum when it comes to food. I love most food – the only thing I won't eat is cheese because I absolutely hate it. Even the smell makes me feel sick. If I have a pizza I have to have it without cheese, which people always find really odd.

Because of being in the band so young I've missed out on learning quite a lot of the stuff you do when you first become independent, like cooking. I've moved into my own place now so I am trying to learn, but I'm not doing brilliantly at the moment.

I've got a perfectly good kitchen at home but I'll still cook Super Noodles for dinner, and I love takeaways. I've got a great Indian restaurant at the end of my road, which is a killer.

Tristan is definitely the worst eater but he's taught himself to cook, so if he can do it, I can. Otherwise I'll end up eating toast and ready meals for the rest of my life.

It is important to look after yourself when you're in a band but I'm not always that great at it. There are times when I'm absolutely knackered, and all you can do is eat well and go to bed early until you feel better. Neither of which I do that often. I'm terrible because if someone suggests we go out I think 'I'll just go out for one' and all of a sudden it's 5 a.m. I've got quite a lot of energy and drinking makes me feel less shy, so I reckon that's part of the reason I think I go a bit crazy.

Being in a band is everything I hoped it would be, but there have also been a hell of a lot of things I wasn't expecting. It's totally exceeded my expectations on so many levels, and surprised me on others.

One thing I didn't realise is how much is involved, from travelling to interviews. I totally underestimated it. I'm definitely not moaning, but I'd only ever seen it from an outside point of view and seen the bands I love having a cool time so I thought it would be all fun and games.

I didn't even think about having to do interviews, radio tours and crazily early mornings. I thought we'd be on tour all the time having a laugh. And we do, but we're also aware that we've got a job to do. If you've got to be up at 6 a.m. for work you can't go out until 4 a.m. and expect to still do a good job the following day, so that's kind of gone out of the window. I do still go out, and I'm not always the most sensible member of the band, but I make sure I never let anything affect our performances.

I do get homesick occasionally and there are times when we're away for a long period of time I really want my own bed and to see my family. I sometimes take my own pillow away with me on tour because it feels like a little bit of home. I started doing that after I had the panic attack because it provided a bit of a comfort.

Even if we're on a massive tour we always know we're going home at the end of it so it's all about having a laugh while we're doing it. I want to enjoy everything we're doing as much as I possibly can. Even our early days of staying in not-so-nice hotels and travelling in the back of a van were fun, and you should always appreciate the moment you're in instead of looking ahead for the next thing.

I've already learnt so much from being in the music industry. I think you have to experience some of the stuff to really get your head around it, but we pay attention to everything that's going on and we're very involved in any decisions that are made about the band.

Before The Vamps I had no idea how many people work behind the scenes at record companies and TV and radio stations, so that's surprised me, but we've met so many amazing people.

I'm friends with the guys from All Time Low now, and we know Ed Sheeran too, and obviously the McFly and Busted boys are so cool. I think everyone in the industry gets on well because we're all going through the same kind of things so we've got a lot to chat about.

We also met Hillary Clinton when we went to Radio 2 last year and she knew who we were. We got introduced and she said to us: 'So *you're* The Vamps, are you?' How the hell does Hillary Clinton know who we are?

I feel like I can still live a relatively normal life generally, even though a lot more people know who I am these days. I mean, I wouldn't go to the Bullring in Birmingham just as the schools empty out, and I did end up locked in a McDonald's toilet once because there were loads of fans outside, but you just have to pick your moments.

We're definitely recognised more when we're together but I like having the other boys with me because it means we can chat to fans together. Even after all this time I still get a bit nervous around people I don't know sometimes.

I'm very lucky because I know that all the people around me are really trustworthy. My friends are the same mates I've had since I was young and I know they would never be interested in talking to the

press about me or selling stories. The only thing that wasn't great was when a guy I know told the *Birmingham Mail* where I live and they printed a photo of the outside of the building. I'd only just moved in so I was gutted.

The tricky thing is meeting new people because I guess you don't always know what someone's motives are. I'm pretty reserved anyway, but I probably just take things a bit more slowly when I'm getting to know people now.

I'm really happy with the friends I already have anyway, and I'm not about to start trying to make loads of new friends in the industry just for the sake of having 'celebrity mates'. I'll always be tight with my real friends, and if I make more along the way that's a bonus.

We've been to some brilliant events since we started out, and personally I really enjoyed the Scottish Fashion Awards because I won a Fashion Icon award. The other boys found it hilarious, and so did I. But Scottish people have got such pride in their country so I think that helped with the votes.

The Radio 1 Teen Awards last year were amazing too. We won three awards – Best British Group, Friday Download Best British Breakthrough Award and Best British Single for 'Last Night' – which is crazy. We didn't expect that at all and we headlined as well. I'm basically naming places where we've won awards, aren't I?

So, as I mentioned at the beginning of the chapter, I'm a bit accident prone so I've injured myself a few times while we've been performing.

The first time was when I fell at the O2 when we were supporting Taylor Swift. I walked right off the end of the stage and ended up crashing to the floor. I lay there laughing for what seemed like ages while this security guard stared down at me.

I got back up and carried on with the show and although everyone in the O2 saw, somehow the other boys didn't. I was on stage laughing to myself about it and I wasn't in pain at all. I think the adrenalin must have kept me going.

The boys didn't see the video of the fall until afterwards and I think they were all a bit freaked out because it looked really bad.

I almost landed on my face and if I hadn't turned quickly I'd probably have broken my nose again. I've already broken it once playing football when I was a kid and I recently had to have an operation to help with my breathing. So all in all I had a very lucky escape.

And then there's my knee nightmare, which happened in early 2016. I first dislocated my knee on stage in Barcelona the year before but it seemed to pop back in on its own. It left me with a bit of weakness but it seemed fine. It happened a few more times on stage and I kept telling myself it would be OK. I was clearly in a bit of denial because it kept happening and I should have seen a doctor straight away.

Then, when we were in Hong Kong as part of our tour of Asia, we were performing one night and I turned round too quickly and my leg stayed in the same place. I felt a massive crunch and I knew something had popped out of place.

We flew to the Philippines the next day where they did an MRI and they said I had to fly home immediately. As my kneecap had popped out it had ripped the cartilage, which got tangled. There was a big tear behind my kneecap and I needed to have it seen to ASAP because there was no way it was going to magically mend itself.

I was on crutches for a couple of weeks and then I had an operation so I had to take a month off from the band in total. I had to wear a full leg brace, which made it pretty hard to do anything.

I stayed with my parents for the first week and a half and then I went back to my flat to recuperate. I could hardly go out and there was no one to talk to so I ended up watching a ridiculous amount of TV. *Jeremy Kyle* and *Come Dine with Me* just don't have the same appeal when you've watched them for days on end. I was *so* bored and frustrated. It was also horrible seeing the other guys carrying on with the band without me and I really missed being with them.

It did give me some time to sit back and reflect on all the amazing things we've done and how far we've come, though. And it made me think about all the other brilliant things we're going to do in the future ...

JAMES

# 'WE NEVER SIT BACK AND THINK, "YEAH, WE'VE MADE IT."'

It's weird looking back on my younger years now because these days everyone thinks I'm the sensible one in the band. And I guess I am in that I always like to be on time and get things organised. But I wasn't always like that. I gave my parents a fair amount of headaches when I was younger. It was only when I got into my late teens that I began to change and grew into the person I am today.

I was born in Chester but my family moved to Dorset when I was four and that's been my home ever since. My dad is from Manchester and my mum's from Liverpool so I've got really strong ties to the north, and I still class up north as home to a certain extent because my extended family are all there.

We moved to Dorset because my dad got a job as a transport manager for the local council. My mum is a health visitor and she's worked for the NHS for all of her adult life, and they've passed on a really strong work ethic to me.

I don't remember a lot about Chester but my earliest ever memories are of going to a place called Betws-y-Coed in Wales when I was about three. I used to love trains and diggers and I got to sit on a little steam train on that holiday. I remember really clearly how excited I was about it.

I also remember when my parents were selling their house in Chester and me and my cousin Oliver, who was three years older than me, put a hose through the letterbox and flooded the porch on the day people were coming round to look at it. We also threw mud at the windows and on to the front of the house, and my parents were really cross. I think we must have been protesting because neither Oliver nor I wanted me to move away.

I kind of blame that incident on Oliver because he was older than me. I don't know if his naughtiness had an effect on me or whether I was just spirited, but I definitely became quite a troublesome child.

I was never horrible or spiteful; I was just quite cheeky and my parents were always threatening to send me up north to live with my aunt and uncle if I didn't behave. That always shut me up for a little while, but as soon as I felt like I was out of the danger zone I'd start messing around again.

I remember hassling my mum to buy me sweets all the time. I loved pick and mix so every time we passed a shop that sold them I'd beg her to buy me some, and I'd shout if she didn't. I was so annoying she usually gave in, and as a result I became pretty overweight.

It didn't help that I couldn't do much exercise. I was terrible at running and didn't really enjoy any other sports at school, but it wasn't until later on that we discovered I had asthma. A combination of little moving around and a lot of sweets meant I was chubby for quite a long time.

From the ages of about six until eleven I talked *a lot* and I was pretty argumentative. I thought I was more intelligent than I was so I'd backtalk the teachers and seek attention from the other children. Maybe it was because I was self-conscious about my weight, but I didn't bother to focus on work and I was more interested in getting a laugh.

I used to get detention for talking in class, mainly to girls, who I slowly started to realise weren't as horrible as I used to think they were. I used to try to impress them, and chatting to them was much more fun than doing work.

Weirdly, I was quite regimented with homework, I guess because there wasn't anything to distract me, so that was the only thing I worked hard on, which meant my grades stayed relatively average.

I was about ten or eleven when I decided I properly wanted to do music, but I couldn't actually play anything and I didn't sing, so I wasn't off to a great start. Then, one Christmas, my dad randomly brought down a guitar from the loft he'd made when he was a teenager, and I decided to have a go on it. The strings were rusty and I had no idea what I was doing, but I was so determined to master it I played until my fingers bled (this isn't some fantasy rock 'n' roll story. They actually did!).

After a few weeks of bleeding fingers my parents could see I was genuinely keen to learn so they bought a really cheap electric guitar to try out. I tried to teach myself to play in my bedroom, but I soon realised it wasn't an easy thing to figure out by yourself so I went and had a couple of lessons.

Once I'd learnt the basics I went away and did the rest on my own, and by the time I was twelve I was pretty much self-taught. I won't pretend I turned into a guitar genius overnight and I'm still learning every day, but I tried my best and I was dedicated and put the work in.

I learnt a few chords and a handful of songs using tab sheet music on the Internet, and when my friend Jonny got given a drum kit for Christmas we started doing (probably hilariously bad) jamming sessions together.

I met some other guys at school who were also trying to play music, and the four of us would regularly get together in a room and play music not very well.

If I'm being totally honest I'm not a natural guitar player, and even now I find it technically difficult to do new things. Connor is brilliant at technical guitar playing, but I learnt simple chords and played rhythm guitar for a long time so I didn't try any of the harder stuff until I was older.

I started to push the boundaries more and more as I got into my mid-teens, but it took me ages to get the hang of doing chords and singing at the same time. It took a lot of perseverance for me to get that right, but once I did I was fine.

It's strange because there's no strong link to music in my background. I got really into bands from watching Saturday morning TV and music channels like MTV and The Box, before YouTube came along and turned everything on its head.

Like Tristan, I really liked Busted. Theirs was the first album I bought and I used to listen to it on my CD Walkman constantly. They were the first band I got really into and I thought everything they did was amazing.

It was also listening to the music my dad played that got me really into bands. He was into groups like Del Amitri and Crowded House when I was really little, and I still remember the lyrics to all of their songs now.

When I was about seven or eight my dad started to listen to stuff like Iron Maiden, which I think is why I started to like rockier music. His taste definitely had an influence on me growing up, and even now to a certain extent.

There are pockets of musical memory throughout my childhood, and one album I'll never be able to forget is Travis's *The Invisible Band*. When I was eleven we went to holiday to France and rented a car. That was the only CD in there so we listened to it over and over again, and even now when I hear a song from that album it takes me back to that time.

Around the same time that I got into Busted I discovered Good Charlotte, and I was fascinated by the fact that the guitarist used to put wood glue in his hair. I'd never seen that whole punk thing before and I thought they were really cool and different. That then led me on to liking other bands who were on the same scene, like Simple Plan, and that started to influence the way I dressed.

I looked totally different back then. These days I tend to stick to wearing jeans, T-shirts, hoodies and trainers (I like to keep things simple). But in my teens I wore black clothes, chains and big trainers. I got my nose pierced when I was fifteen, and then shortly afterwards I got flesh holes in my ears. My mum hated them and she always used to say to me: 'I can see the kitchen cupboards through your ears.' Thankfully they healed up pretty well and it's hard to tell I ever had them now.

I guess I was just rebelling like teenagers do and I got it all out of my system pretty quickly. Thankfully I was never into drugs, alcohol or smoking. And I didn't get any dodgy tattoos. I do think about getting

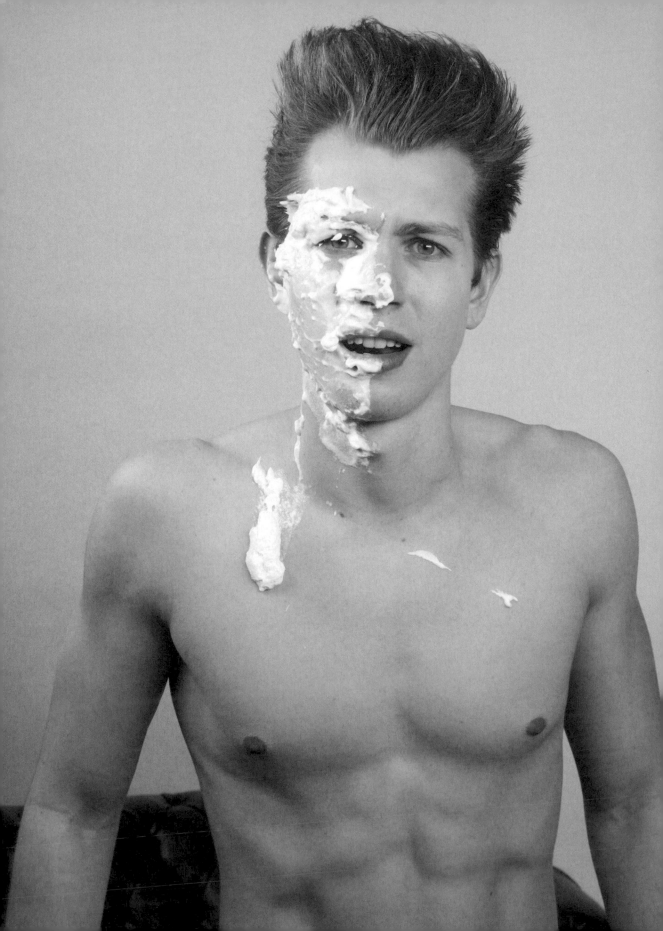

a tattoo some day, but I can't decide what I'd like so it's best to wait until I'm completely sure. Unless you want to go through some really painful removal you've got a tattoo for life, so you need to be 100 per cent certain you're still going to like it, or at least appreciate it, in ten years' time.

I found my early teens quite difficult in some ways. All of my friends I was at middle school with went to grammar school when I was eleven, and I didn't so I lost touch with a lot of people. I'd been hanging around with the same bunch of friends for years so I felt a bit lost, and when I started high school I didn't know many people.

I also developed really bad acne, which didn't do a lot for my confidence. It may sound strange but I found having acne intimidating and it made me nervous about meeting new people. I always felt like people were looking at my spots and not really listening to what I was saying when I spoke to them, and because of that I became a bit introverted for a while.

I tried everything to get rid of my spots over the years, but it wasn't until I was put on Accutane when I was nineteen that they finally cleared up. I still get spots every now and again, and I'm really vocal about it on social media because I know how hard it can be for people.

I know how much it affected me so I want people to know that they're not the only ones who suffer. I felt like I was the only person in the world with bad skin – which of course I *wasn't* – and it made me really self-conscious.

Now I realise that imperfections are what make us who we are and make us different and interesting, and I embrace my flaws. But when you're fourteen and you have a face covered with pimples it's not so easy to see things that way.

Because I was really open about the fact I wanted to do music as a career some people thought I was a bit weird and didn't take me seriously. I guess every young guy wants to be in a band at some point, so it seemed a bit ridiculous.

So all in all, in my early teens I dressed weirdly, I had spots, I was into music and I didn't have many friends, so I didn't really feel like I fitted in. I didn't have many mates, and there were times when I felt quite alone. Music was what gave me a focus and a goal.

My salvation came in the form of a band called Negative Response (catchy), which I started with a few guys from school. At first we tried learning cover songs but we found it really confusing, so we started making up our own songs using just a few chords. It was really basic but in hindsight it taught me something about musicianship and introduced me to songwriting in its simplest form.

We were only about thirteen or fourteen but we played for the school a couple of times and we did a couple of gigs here and there, but I don't think any of us ever thought it was going to lead to anything big. We didn't ever properly click, and it wasn't anything like when The Vamps first started out because that felt so instant.

When I was about fourteen I started to get properly interested in girls and my behaviour at school started to improve. I went from messing around in class to get girls' attention to actually wanting a girlfriend.

I used to go to local youth clubs and I met loads of girls there, and despite being a bit chubby with bad skin, my awkward, under-confident approach seemed to work. I became the first one out of all my mates to start going out with someone and that gave me a bit of a boost. I don't know if the whole music thing helped, but despite not feeling like the most 'normal' guy in the world I seemed to do OK with the opposite sex.

Negative Response lived up to their name because when I asked the other band members if I could sing more I got kicked out the band. So when I was about fifteen or sixteen I began doing acoustic music on my own and writing songs with a summery feel. That's when I developed an element of artistry and I was getting to the point where I could write a complete song.

My music tastes shifted a bit around this time and I started listening to music by Damien Rice, The Kooks and The Goo Goo Dolls, who all had a massive influence on me. I started playing some local gigs to get experience and despite still being a bit shy, I found that I loved being in front of an audience.

MySpace was massive around this time, and I saved up all my money and paid for a couple of hours in a recording studio so I could record some songs. I put the results on MySpace and sent my songs off to different people. I started to get more gigs around the UK off the back of that, and I went to London a couple of times to perform, which was very exciting at that age. There's a video still on YouTube of my first real trip to London, from when I appeared on something called Balcony TV. Check out the hair!

I played a gig in Birmingham with Diana Vickers about six years ago. She was headlining a show outside a shopping centre and a guy called Liam Payne and I supported her.

Liam was doing solo stuff like me at the time and we stayed in touch for a few months afterwards, but then I changed my phone and lost his number and I haven't seen or spoken to him since. But he's done pretty well for himself since then, hasn't he? It would be nice to chat or bump into him again sometime because we got on really well.

My parents were really supportive of me performing and doing gigs but they were never pushy. Because I was a bit nervous about doing it, my mum would phone up venues on my behalf and ask if I could do a gig there. I managed to get some regular slots and I become pretty well known around Dorset.

I was happy as a solo artist but I sort of plateaued when it came to gigging, and I felt like I'd done everything I could back home. I knew that if I wanted to take it to the next level I had to spread my wings. I enjoyed writing songs but I never saw myself as a lead singer, so I started to wonder if I'd be more suited to being in a band. But I still wasn't sure if I could have a serious future in music.

I was the only Vamp to have jobs when I was growing up. After I finished my GCSEs (despite not exactly applying myself I got an A*, four As, two Bs and four Cs, although I always thought I could have done better) I got a couple of waiting jobs in cafés. And after that I got a job in the flagship Animal store in Dorset. I worked there for about nine months in total and the team were great but it showed me I didn't want a job like that full time. That inspired me to push for more, and when I started sixth form I told myself I needed to work hard and do well in my A levels.

Things really changed for me at sixth form. After feeling like I didn't really fit in when I was at school, I met loads of new people and made friends really easily. I started going out with the head girl and because she was really studious it rubbed off on me.

I also started getting into fitness and the gym, and after being overweight for so long it was a bit of a revelation. I started to really feel like myself at last, and it was like I began to discover who I really was. Taking care of myself had a knock-on effect with everything else, and for the first time ever I felt like I could do anything I put my mind to.

It helped that I had a double focus at sixth form. I was working on my A levels in English Literature, History and Applied Science in lunch and break times, and even after school in the library. But I was also still doing a lot of music on the side. I was really busy, but really happy.

When I met Brad, the music stepped up a gear and that's when I kind of knew I wasn't going to end up going to university. I probably would have ended up studying journalism or English, but by the time I was eighteen I knew I wanted to make music my priority and if I'd gone to uni I would have totally drifted. What was the point in wasting that time?

I left sixth form with two 2A*s and an A, which I was really happy about, so I knew at least I had the qualifications I needed if I did decide I wanted to go to uni later down the line.

I'm so grateful I discovered fitness at that time. Things like going to the gym and eating healthily really help me if things get crazy with the band nowadays.

I'm the complete opposite to the sweet-eating kid I once was, and I try to live the healthiest lifestyle possible. It's something I feel like I can have an element of control over when everything else is all over the place.

It's hard when I'm on tour because often we have to grab things in service stations, but when I'm at home I cook everything from scratch so I know what's in it. I've been vegetarian since last Christmas and I'm not yet sure if it's a lifetime thing or not, but I'm enjoying it.

Going to the gym is great because it's so good for releasing tension and it's something I can do pretty consistently. But equally I can get a bit stressed if I don't have time to go. So I guess sometimes it winds me up too. But I absolutely couldn't do without it. Sometimes the other boys will come with me if we're away, mainly Brad or Connor, and there has been the odd occasion when we've managed to drag Tristan along.

The four of us are still really normal guys and we never sit back and think, 'Yeah, we're famous. We've made it.' We're still the same people we've always been. We don't think we're cooler or better than we were three years ago. If one of us ever did get big-headed we'd totally rein them in.

We still get excited about things and appreciate everything, and being in the band wouldn't be as much fun if we didn't. Flying business class on planes is still such a novelty for us, and if we turn up and see a crowd outside a venue it still feels incredible. We'll never take that kind of thing for granted.

There wasn't one point where I stopped and thought, 'Wow, I'm famous.' In fact I don't class myself as famous because I still get on the tube most days I'm in London and don't get recognised. We've got a nice level of fame and we're really lucky we can lead pretty 'normal' lives.

Day to day I do try to keep a certain amount of my life private, and I find that pretty easy because our fans are so respectful. I make sure I don't tweet about where I'm going if I'm having quiet family time. I love hanging out with my family because it's so easy and chilled-out.

I've got a little sister called Sophie who is fifteen, and the age gap is quite peculiar because if we were only a few years apart we probably would have done more stuff together when we were growing up. But we're very close now and we text and tweet each other a lot.

Sophie was quite shy when she was younger but she's come out of her shell more in the past few years, which is good because it must be quite strange having a brother who's in a band. It's all she's ever known but I think it's only in the past couple of years she's become more conscious of what's going on.

I think what I do means she's pretty popular at school sometimes, but I do worry about people being jealous and there's a danger they could be unkind. But she's got a really solid, close group of friends who aren't in the least bit fussed about what I do, which is great. Thanks, Katy and Natasha!

I definitely feel like I can still make a choice about how much I want to be recognised and how much I want to stay under the radar. I get recognised quite a lot back home because everyone knows each other, and there are certain places that I'm better off not going to.

I went to a Union J concert a couple of years ago just after our album came out and I got asked to leave the venue by the security. I ended up locked in the toilet with 200 people waiting outside, which was pretty scary. My friend Adam acted as impromptu security but, in the end, we both had to run for our lives!

If I went to a busy shopping centre at the weekend with the other guys I would be asking to get recognised, but when I'm walking around London day-to-day no one cares.

The weirdest place I get recognised is probably in the gym back home. My gym is next to a girls' grammar school and somehow they always find out when I'm there. It's strange when you're lifting weights and you turn around to find loads of pairs of eyes and camera phones watching you.

I don't mind being recognised at all, but it can be quite stressful if we're running late and we have to be somewhere. We were at a radio station recently and people tweeted me afterwards saying they were annoyed I didn't stop to chat, but I was booked on a train home to see my family and I would have missed it if I hadn't run straight into a car. I always stop if I can because I love talking to our fans, but sometimes I don't have a choice.

The only negatives about being in The Vamps for me are being away from home and not being able to have a routine. I know the other boys don't mind it but it's a big thing for me. Even being able to go to the gym when I've planned to can be tricky because our schedule changes so much. But the positives outweigh the negatives a million times over. How many people can say they've travelled the world twice?

Being in the band has also enabled me to meet some amazing people. I'd been a fan of Taylor Swift since I was fifteen and then we got to go on tour with her, which is crazy.

I was eighteen when we first met her at Radio 1's Teen Awards and I was properly starstruck. I literally couldn't speak. The other boys chatted away but I was shaking. I'd never experienced what it was like to meet someone I was a proper fan of until that moment and it was *so* weird.

I knew Ed Sheeran a bit before he made it really big, and we got back in touch again recently via Twitter. I did a cover of 'The A Team' in 2009 and sent it to him to watch. The song hadn't even been released properly so you could only hear it on YouTube, and he replied saying he couldn't check it out because he didn't have a laptop. I think he was living on a sofa at that point!

I didn't speak to him again for years and then I randomly tweeted him about six months before our first album came out. He replied suggesting we write together at some point, and needless to say I'd love to. He's insanely talented.

His first album, +, was so massive, and he invited me to listen to his second album, x, in a private studio in London before it was released. Tristan came along too, and it was just me, Tris, Ed and a studio technician listening to it together, and I knew straight away how insanely big it was going to go. It was so cool.

I'm pretty friendly with Sam Smith now as well, which is strange because I'm a big fan of his, too. We started tweeting each other and then he invited me along to his Brixton show last year, and we've kept in touch ever since.

I'm probably the most active on social media in the band, and I do like to share a lot because I think it's a big part of what we do. I also love it because it's given me relationships with people and I see a real reward from that interaction.

I agree that there can be a lot of negativity around social media, but I think if it's used in the right way it can harness great things. Without social media I doubt we would be where we are now because we developed and progressed simply through people tweeting and sharing our covers. It was fundamental for us.

I do get trolled quite a lot and various things we've said have been misinterpreted so we can get given a hard time. But you have to accept it because it's part of the job. We didn't get any hate for the first year we were around but there came a point where, in a weirdly positive way, we got big enough to get hate!

In the beginning I found it really hard to deal with and I'd rise to the bait and reply to people. But now I've got to a point where I laugh. I try to picture what these people are like and remember that they don't actually *know* us. They may not like a song but it's not us *personally* they're attacking. If someone is really offensive I'll block them, but otherwise I let it go over my head.

I have to remember that Twitter isn't real and enjoy it for what it is. Someone will send me hate one day and love the next. I'll see someone who has said something horrible to me on Twitter standing outside a radio station and they'll be really nice. Then they'll send me hate the next day again. There's no rhyme or reason to it so it's best not to analyse it. It's not constructive for me to take it on.

We're very lucky because some other band's fans can't stand each other and have wars on social media, but ours seem to get on fine. Sometimes there's a bit of a mob mentality where one person starts having a go so another one does, but generally they're brilliant.

We're constantly meeting new people, whether it's fans or journalists or people who work in TV, and I used to find that really nerve-wracking but I've got used to it now.

I've learnt to read people better over time. This industry is amazing, but it can attract pretty shallow people. Some people you meet are always smiling and joking around and it's a bit fake; you can tell there's no depth there. I remember speaking to one girl – who has since gone on to become a really famous model – for several months just after our first album dropped. I was still very new to the industry so I was flattered when she told me she wanted to be with me.

Then I saw some pictures of her in the press partying on Justin Bieber's yacht and suddenly she cut all ties with me. That's when I realised that not all the people in my new world were genuine. Some people are constantly trying to climb the fame ladder to get to the next level. They make out that their whole world is incredible and they're always happy, but it's a façade because no one is really like that all the time.

I can definitely spot people who aren't genuine and who wouldn't care about knowing me if I wasn't in The Vamps. There are a lot of people who try to latch on but I know who my real friends are, and I'm always up for building more genuine relationships.

I've met so many brilliant people who don't have an agenda or a reason to be nice to me, and you just have to try and take the good out of every situation. We're in an incredible position and we meet some incredible characters.

I've made some friends who will be with me for life, including the other three boys, and I consider myself incredibly lucky.

# 'I GOT "KINDLY ASKED" TO LEAVE MY PRIMARY SCHOOL.'

It's crazy to think how different my life would have been if I'd never picked up a pair of drumsticks when I was a kid. I honestly have no idea what I'd be doing now if I hadn't got into music. Can you be a professional *FIFA* player?

I was born in Hammersmith, London where my dad worked as an independent financial advisor and my mum was an air hostess. My brother James came along first, and I followed a year later. I've also got a younger sister called Millie, who's ten, and I swear she's already much cooler than me.

My parents were living in a one-bedroom flat when James and I were young and there wasn't enough space for four humans, so when I was three they decided to move to Somerset so they could have more room.

We moved to a farm and my earliest memories are of living there. Even though I was only three I remember being aware of how quiet it was, and we had so much space to run around in compared to London.

It was once a proper working farm, and while we didn't have cows or sheep in the fields, we did have horses. I used to ride a lot when I was younger, and my mum and I used to go on riding holidays to Spain together. I still ride now when I get the chance and I love it.

We also had a goat and a guinea pig, but that got eaten by the blacksmith's dog. I remember coming home from school when I was about eight and my mum said to me: 'You're not going to like this ... '

We stayed at the farm until I was twelve and then we moved to Exeter in Devon and lived literally in the middle of nowhere. In some ways it was a great place to grow up because it was beautiful and we had so many different places to go out and play in, but it was six miles away

from the nearest bus stop so there wasn't an awful lot to do. I think that's why I love London so much now. Peace and quiet is great when you're a certain age, but when you reach your teens you want to be around people doing new things and I felt like I was missing out on that.

I've lived in London for a while now and I still find it awesome that I've got a phone signal, decent internet and a supermarket just down the road, because I didn't have those things growing up. When I first joined The Vamps I used to get really excited about seeing supermarkets everywhere and the other boys found it hilarious. I was like the shop spotter and I used to point them out every time we passed one. No one can say I'm not fun to travel with.

I loved growing up around nature and I really appreciated being brought up in such a lovely place, but I don't think I could go back to living there now. I get bored in the countryside.

Having said that, when we go off travelling and places are really built-up and noisy it makes me realise how beautiful Devon is and how lucky I was to be surrounded by endless fields and to have so much freedom as a child.

But I think I was always destined to live in London and even when I was younger I loved visiting and smelling the fumes and being a part of the busyness. My dad used to take James and me on a trip to London every six months so we could do cool stuff like go to the theatre or to the museums. That may not sound like that much fun to a lot of people, but I didn't have any of that back home so it was a real novelty to me.

Our closest neighbour lived over a mile away so I didn't get to see my mates much – if at all – but I was really close to my brother. We still get on well now and I think because we're so close in age we went through a lot of things at similar times and we had the same kind of interests. I'm sure I was an annoying younger brother at times, but siblings always get on each other's nerves, don't they?

We did have an entire year when we didn't speak to each other at all, though. We went through some kind of weird phase when I was about thirteen where we didn't communicate at all. We'd sit down to breakfast and totally ignore each other. I don't even think we properly fell out over anything; we just used to wind each other up a lot and have ridiculous fights. But eventually we both got bored of it and decided to be mates again.

My brother was an actor when he was younger and he appeared in *Casualty* and *Holby City* when he was nine, and he was involved with Stagecoach. But there came a point where he didn't want to act any more and he totally changed directions career-wise. He's now in charge of logistics at a private jet company, which is a cool job.

School was pretty good but I'm not going to lie, I was a tricky student. I got 'kindly asked' to leave my primary school because I was a bit of a brat. I like to think I was just energetic, but actually I was really naughty.

I was never nasty but I was always getting into trouble and I used to nick the other kids' Pokémon cards, which didn't make me very popular at times. But how else are you supposed to get a complete set? (I know, I know. It was a bad thing to do.)

When I got kicked out of school, instead of sending me to another local primary, my parents decided to send me to a private school in Tiverton. Because the classes were much smaller and the teachers were able to dedicate more time to each pupil they hoped they'd be able to teach me to channel my energy in more constructive ways. And, to be fair, it worked. I started to actually enjoy school and made loads of new friends.

I wonder if part of the reason I played up so much when I was really young was because I struggled with the academic side of things. I was always really creative, and my school helped to nurture that. I got the opportunity to do more art and music, which I think is what saved me from going completely off the rails.

There were only eight people in the class so I was also able to concentrate more and get away with less. I reckon if I hadn't gone to that school I would have ended up on a permanent detention somewhere else. But I had no choice but to stop acting like an idiot because the teachers could keep an eye on me at all times. I was kind of forced into not being incredibly irritating.

Although I did well in creative subjects I found it hard to concentrate on anything I wasn't interested in, and so I didn't do very well in exams. My mind was always thinking about a hundred different things, and at no point was one of them equations. I never liked the idea of living my life through a textbook and learning everything by reading from a page. I wanted to go out and experience things.

I hated maths, but although I wasn't very good at biology, I found it really interesting so I did at least learn something from those classes. Aside from that I was all about drama, art and music. Looking back I wish I'd paid more attention to history as well because now I'm older it's something I really like, and that's a big part of the reason I enjoy travelling so much. I love discovering new things, and while I'm not as good as James at going sightseeing when we're away, I do like to learn about the local culture if I get a chance.

School was amazing generally, but I reckon I've learnt so much more about life/the world/random stuff since joining the band and experiencing things. When I was younger I could never have imagined myself sitting in a board meeting, but now we do that all the time with our record company, and we have loads of input in everything. That alone has taught me a lot of new skills.

School can teach you how to pass a history test, but when you visit places like the Tower of London or the Colosseum in Rome you pick up loads of stuff without even trying.

When we went to an event at St James's Palace there was so much history on the walls and I couldn't stop looking at everything. There were all these paintings and weapons that were worth fortunes, and you can't get the feel of those kinds of things from a book. I'm not suggesting that everyone goes to look at swords in royal buildings, but I do think it's a much more interesting way to expand your mind.

I did learn tons at school too, and I'm so grateful I went to such a good one. I think because my teachers were strict and didn't let me get away with anything I'm really good at taking constructive criticism now I'm older, which is important. I also don't mind being told what to do (even if I don't always do it).

I think you need rules as a kid, and the fear of letting my parents down helped to keep me on track. They were working so hard to put me through school and it would have been awful if I'd been kicked out of there too.

So where did the drumming come in? I guess it was always kind of there in one way or another. From the age of seven I used to get told off for humming in class and banging on the table all the time (who knew that being noisy and annoying could lead to a career?).

Because I was quite frenetic, my parents and teachers both suggested I found an outlet for my excess energy, and that happened to be drumming. As soon as I started playing I loved it, and finding something I was good at meant I was happy to put in the hours learning as much as I could.

To begin with, drumming was just a hobby and something I did at school as and when I could, but when I got my first drum kit aged nine I started taking it more seriously.

I became part of the school marching band and I really enjoyed it. I was lucky enough to be the tipper, which is the main drummer, and I could tell my parents were really proud, which meant a hell of a lot to me.

Stick work is really important in drumming and I worked on that for two years while I was in the drum corps, which gave me a real advantage when I started playing kit drums. People started telling me I was really good and that encouraged me to keep going. And thank God I did.

It may sound dramatic but drumming is what kept me on the straight and narrow. It gave me a focus and kept me off the mean streets of Exeter! I probably would have ended up drinking in parks with mates in my early teens, but instead all my attention was on music.

Obviously I didn't realise back then that drumming could be something I could do as a career, but my school was really encouraging and totally supported me. They could all see that I was taking it seriously and I worked really, really hard at it. Even my headmaster loved it. I think my life would be very different if I hadn't discovered drumming.

I had drumming lessons every Friday after school an hour's drive away from our house. My poor parents had to ferry me back and forth every week, and if they hadn't done that there's no way I could have carried on.

There were times when I was due to go to a lesson and all I wanted to do was laze around at home and watch TV, and it was my mum and dad who gave me a kick up the arse and made me go to my lessons, even though it was a pain for them.

Quite often it was my dad who used to drive me to lessons and it was good bonding time. We had some really good chats on those journeys, and it was nice because you don't always spend that much time with your parents when you're young.

My dad listened to a lot of dance music in the car when I was growing up and I always really liked the hooks of the songs, so that had a big influence on me. I was always more into hooks than actual lyrics because I loved the sounds and hearing how the chorus changed. The feel of it was more appealing to me than the actual songwriting.

The first band I was really into was the brilliant Busted (and I used to really fancy Avril Lavigne). But when I started buying albums it was always pop-punk type stuff like Green Day and Blink 182, and I thought I was so cool.

From the age of twelve I flexi-boarded at my school because I wanted to hang out with my friends as much as possible. My school looked like Hogwarts and we had dorms so it was like a massive sleepover. We'd play sports and mess about and pop into town to go shopping (another time I used to get excited about supermarkets).

Flexi-boarding meant I could stay at school two or three nights a week and go home and see my family when I wanted to, so I had the best of both worlds.

I was in a lot of bands at school and we used to rehearse most afternoons. I'd just start jamming with people and see how it went. I was also in bands outside of school so I juggled quite a lot at times, but it was what gave me a really good starting point musically.

I joined a band called Leave Before Dawn when I was about fourteen and the rest of the band were all in their late twenties. We used to do pub gigs and little tours with other friends of mine who were in bands. Because I was so young my dad had to drive me around to these really crappy places, and even though some of the venues were awful I really liked getting experience.

The worst gigs I ever did were in pubs where hardly anyone turned up. I remember travelling all the way to a pub in Falmouth, which took forever, and when we arrived there were three people in the entire place, including the barman. I probably got paid about £20 and it would have cost my dad more than that in petrol to get me there.

Because at that time I didn't realise I could make a living out of being a drummer, I had no idea what I wanted to do when I was a grown up (I'm still waiting for that to happen).

I had a really negative view of work and I thought I'd end up with a crappy job when I was older, so I might as well enjoy myself before that happened.

The education system makes you feel like if you don't do well academically there isn't much out there for you. And I knew I was never going to be the guy who did a mainstream degree at university and then landed a top job.

Even though I was at a school that encouraged creativity I still wasn't pushed towards any kind of solid career, so I felt quite confused about my future for a while.

I didn't consider that the thing I was most passionate about could morph into my career one day. My parents were really encouraging when I said I wanted to be a drummer but I'm not sure even they – my biggest supporters – were convinced I could make a proper go of it.

It's funny because sometimes you can take the things you're good at for granted. Some people are really good at writing poetry or short stories but they don't consider they could do that as a job because it feels more like a hobby. I think you should play to your strengths and do things that a) you're good at and b) you enjoy. It's so much nicer if work isn't a massive slog, and the only way to make that happen is to do something you like.

I was so busy with music at school that I wasn't that interested in girls until I got a bit older. I was popular when I was in year eight, and then in year nine puberty kicked in and I became really shy and self-conscious.

I didn't meet my first girlfriend until I was at college, but we were together for three years, right up until I joined The Vamps. She ended up going to university up north and with me travelling so much it made things really difficult, so eventually we split up.

I left school still feeling a bit confused about my future. I passed ten of my eleven GCSEs so I did better than I thought I would, and I only failed the other one because I managed to miss the exam (don't ask). I decided to go to the Academy of Music and Sound in Exeter. It wasn't really what I wanted to be doing because I was keen to break into the music business there and then, but I didn't know how. I needed to stay in education, so music college seemed like the best option. It was almost like a babysitting course while I decided what my next step was going to be.

College was quite a shock and gave me a totally different perspective on things. It was the polar opposite of my private school and I met loads of new people from different backgrounds. I guess I'd been pretty sheltered living in the country and part-boarding, and it was a real eye-opener. It changed a lot for me personally.

I turned up on my first day wearing white jeans and you could spot me a mile off because I was the only one wearing them. I soon learnt not to do that.

I made a load of new friends and I honestly think I became a lot more rounded during my time there. I also met a couple of dudes called Peter and Joe who were really into music like me, and we started a band together called Malicious.

When I was sixteen I signed up to a website called StarNow because I thought it would be a good way to meet people and get jobs. I put my details on there and, as a result, I started doing session drumming when I was sixteen. I'd finish college for the day, get on a train to London and do a session, and then get the train home.

Because I'd started drumming so early I'd learnt several different genres like Latin, rock, pop and jazz, which meant I could play for loads of different people.

The first full-on London show I did was at Kensington Roof Gardens and it was so cool. I met loads of interesting people and I felt like I was on the first rung of the music ladder. My plan was to get all the way to the top, and I felt like I'd finally made a start.

I heard about James (McVey, not my brother – that would be weird) through a friend, and I instantly knew that he was on my wavelength. He sounded so similar to me and he was into the same kind of music I was.

I added James on Facebook soon afterwards and we started chatting. He and Brad were already in touch at that time, and I loved the feel of what they were working on.

One of the first things the three of us talked about was getting a black card for Nando's, which basically means you get all your food for free. That was one of our big dreams back then, and we eat *a lot* of chicken now.

The Vamps was something I was massively passionate about and I really wanted to be a part of it, but nothing was guaranteed and I needed a back-up plan. I managed to get a place at the Academy of Contemporary Music in Guildford, where I was going to study business, because I was really interested in the economics side of the industry. I *still* wasn't convinced drumming was going to give me the kind of income I could live on, and my parents wanted me to have something to fall back on as well.

When I did my GCSE music course at school I got to learn about producing, and that was something I was keen to learn more about too. I've always been interested in making beats and producing is just an extension of that. I'm not necessarily the best technically when it comes to music because I don't use chords, but I love the sound, the beat and the structure.

Needless to say I didn't do the course in the end because things started to properly kick off with the band. Maybe this drumming thing is going to work out after all?

Being in a band is kind of what I expected, but also not. I've been in bands for years, but not successful ones, and I didn't realise just how much work was involved.

I'm not afraid to work hard at all, but a lot of people just see the red carpet stuff and the glitz and glamour, and they don't realise that there's a lot of travelling and interviews involved. We have to do press and TV days all around the world, sometimes with terrible jetlag, which I'm not very good at! It's not exactly a hardship though, and we all know what an absolutely incredible opportunity we've been given.

I didn't expect to be able to buy a house at twenty-one, for instance. But none of us are going crazy and throwing money around on stupid things. We've all got our heads screwed on properly and we're not going to be hitting up casinos and chucking around bottles of champagne anytime soon.

The band started getting recognised quite early on because of all the YouTube covers we did. It wasn't like we were being chased down the street but a lot of people started to know who we were. Our fans were really supportive, and we could get a little crowd together if we wanted.

When we went to meet Sony about potentially signing a record deal there were about ten One Direction fans waiting outside. We played an acoustic song for them called 'She Was the One', which became a fan favourite and appeared on the first album. That night the girls set up some Twitter fan accounts for us, and from that moment on things started to build and more and more accounts started up. After that every time we put a song up on YouTube we got loads of views and word started to spread. We were on our way!

We were lucky in a way because we became well known gradually. It wasn't like we were an overnight sensation, and the first time fans turned up to see us we were really taken aback. The support we've had has been unbelievable. The fans are the ones who make you and we say it time and time again – we're so grateful.

We can go out without being mobbed even now because we're sensible about it. If I go out locally where I live I'm unlikely to be recognised, but if I went to Oxford Street during the Easter holidays it would be a different story. So I guess I'm just a bit more aware than I used to be.

If I went out dressed in the kind of outfit I'd wear on stage and had my hair really high I would be asking for people to notice me, but most of the time I look like any other guy my age.

I get a lot of people saying, 'You look like that guy from The Vamps,' because they don't expect it to be me. But it's not like I can't live a normal life. I can still do my own food shopping, which is obviously very important for me.

I would never complain about being recognised because I put myself in this position, and you do have choices. We've shared security with Justin Bieber and I know he still goes down the pub. And if he can, we can!

The only thing I find hard about being in the band sometimes is missing my family. When we have commitments we have to stick to them, and if something is happening at home and I want to be there I can't just drop everything and run back.

My sister is very dependent on her big brothers and every time I see her she seems to have grown. I feel sad that I'm missing that, but I guess that would be the same whatever job I was doing. I'd probably drive her mad if I were there all the time anyway because I annoy her at times. She isn't in any way bothered about me being in a band. Her friends are all really into The Vamps but she's just like 'whatever'.

Sometimes this job can be a bit stressful. There is a bit of pressure to sell records because we're aware of how quickly things could end. But that just makes us more determined to make great music so we can keep doing this for as long as possible. I channel any pressure I feel and it drives me.

The best stress reliever I've found if I am worrying about anything is the other guys. If any of us are feeling a bit down we'll all prop them up. We all love what we do so much and if we didn't it would make this job a hell of a lot harder. In fact, I really don't think we could carry on doing it if we weren't 100 per cent committed.

We laugh at everything as a band. If we released a new album tomorrow and it sold two copies we'd be pissed off but we'd honestly joke about it. We try to get a sense of humour about everything and there's nothing we won't take the mickey out of.

That doesn't mean we're not taking the band seriously because we are, but we're also having the best time. We're in an amazing position and I don't want to look back in ten years' time and think I didn't enjoy it all as much as I could have done.

The craziest thing for me about being in the band is the fact we've played the O2 arena fourteen times. That's like our home venue now.

I've seen all of my favourite bands like Linkin Park and Blink 182 there, and we've actually headlined. It's always the place our friends and family come along to see us as well, so I've got really good memories of being backstage.

Hold on a minute – how ridiculous is that sentence? 'I've got really good memories of being backstage at the O2!' If you'd told fourteen-year-old me I'd be able to say that one day I would have thought you were insane. But God, it feels amazing.

à la française

HITTING THE BIG TIME

TOURING WITH TAYLOR,
DODGY HOTELS AND WHY WE
RUB OUR CHINS TOGETHER
BEFORE A SHOW

**BRAD:** Before we go out on tour we go to a studio in London and we do about two weeks of full-on rehearsals. That involves us getting the set together (the song set – we don't build the actual set), and we record all of the backing tracks and interludes. We don't have a musical director or anything and Tristan takes on most of that role. It takes a bit longer and it's more pressure on us, but we love it.

**TRISTAN:** We have production rehearsals and sort out what we're going to play, and then we go to an arena for two days and sort out the lights and pyros and work out how everything will work with the music. It's wicked.

**JAMES:** We really enjoy coming up with ideas for things, like the runway and fire which both looked wicked on the last tour. The runway was like a catwalk with a small stage at the end so we could get up close and personal with the fans, and that makes the gigs feel more intimate.

**BRAD:** People think that doing a tour is overwhelming but it's like any job you have a deadline for. If you work in IT or finance you'd still have deadlines, and although when we first start working on a tour it feels like there's loads to do, it always comes together.

We love touring and we want to come across as the best live band we can be, so we kind of enjoy that pressure in a way. It's exciting and we're always looking to do something different, so it's a really creative process.

It's also quite relaxed building up to a tour because we have more of a routine so we get to get up later, which obviously I love. We also get to go home to see our families when we tour in the UK, which we all really like too.

**CON:** I missed a lot of the pre-tour preparations last time around because I couldn't get to London due to my knee operation. It's a shame because that rehearsal time is really fun. Tristan does all the production on his laptop and we all come up with ideas.

It takes a lot of people to translate the ideas from the rehearsal studio to venues. There are so many really talented crew members involved.

The support acts we have on tour are usually people we like and get on with, or they're people who are on the same record label as us. We had to throw one band off our Australian tour last year. They were being idiots and running over time every night. They were also swearing at our fans and they slagged off our management on stage. They were trying to be rock 'n' roll but we weren't having any of it.

BRAD: We had the best time ever on the last tour. But every tour we do feels incredible because it's what I've always wanted to do. When I was growing up I had an *AC/DC Live at Donington* DVD and I used to watch it over and over again and think, 'That's what I want to be doing.' It wasn't an ego thing; it just looked like so much fun.

How can I describe that feeling when you first get on stage? I'm not sure if I can. It's just the best. It's hard to explain but everything around you seems to disappear and something takes over.

I won't ever get to the point where I take performing for granted and go through the motions. I like to put on a different gig each night and make sure it's a proper show. It's the small changes that make a gig special.

TRISTAN: Being on stage in an arena is almost too much to take in. When you look out at the crowd it's overwhelming. I can't find the words to describe it because it's so mad. It's almost like it's not happening. I would probably feel more nervous performing for three people than I would 90,000 now because it would be more personal.

People think that because I'm tucked away at the back it's less nerve-wracking, but it's really not. I had a drum solo on our last tour and I was thirty feet in the air. It was just me and the audience, which was pretty exposing but also awesome.

BRAD: Selling out the O2 shows again last time around was unreal and the concerts themselves were wicked. We always tweak things after the first couple of shows, and by the time we got to the O2 we felt like it was really slick. Tom Daley, Ben Phillips, Caspar Lee, Joe Sugg and Katie Price all came along, and so did all our families.

**JAMES:** We do meet and greets on the tour, which is great because we get to meet loads of new fans as well as see ones we've known for a long time. We have pictures taken with everyone and have a chat, and generally we see about 150 people at each venue.

It's so nice because it means we can get around to everyone and spend time with them, which you can't always do when you're doing a radio interview or something. Fans also give us presents, and it can be anything from jumpers to books to face masks (my dream). Our fans are amazing because they really take their time to find out what we like and we're pretty spoilt to be fair. So thank you!

**CON:** It's rare for us to have a routine in the band, but we do when we're on tour. We get up, have breakfast together and go to the gym (well, not Tristan). Then we sound check, play ping-pong, do the show, and have drinks afterwards and go out if we want to.

**TRISTAN:** We've been so lucky that we've got to tour with The Wanted, McFly, Taylor Swift and Selena Gomez, and we've also played show with artists like Jessie J, Little Mix, Labrinth and Tinie Tempah.

**CON:** Touring was Taylor was incredible. She'd watched our cover of her song '22' on YouTube and that was what made her want us to support her. That's crazy, isn't it? She was watching *us*!

It was ridiculous when we found out she wanted us to support her. James was the most shocked because he absolutely loves her, but we were all stunned because she's the biggest artist in the world. And then I fell off the stage at her show. *Brilliant.*

**JAMES:** Taylor had a dressing room get-together at the end of her tour and she invited us along. At the end of the night it was just us, Cara Delevingne, Taylor and two of her backing dancers chatting away.

It was so peculiar because I was with one of my idols having a laugh like it was the most normal thing in the world. Everyone was having drinks and messing about, and at one point Cara was teaching Connor how to do yoga.

We love sharing the stage with other artists. If we're doing a big show everyone tends to hang out backstage so you get to catch up with people you know.

Even though we're sometimes headlining the shows we still get starstruck when we see the other acts. We went to a party at a club after the Capital FM Jingle Bell Ball last year and Justin Bieber, Ellie Goulding and Nick Jonas were there and I was like, 'What are we doing here?' It's at times like those where I don't feel like I belong, even though we'd just played a concert alongside them.

BRAD: Touring the UK is very different to touring abroad. We've covered the whole of America and Canada, which often involves twelve-hour drives between venues. We're all together in a small space so we spend *a lot* of time together.

The tour buses we have are so cool. The first time we went on one it was all so alien to us and we couldn't believe it because it was like a house. The American buses we've had are single decker, and Tristan likes that because he can stand up in them.

The US ones have got beds and a living room and we'll set up a studio in the back lounge. The UK buses have usually got a lounge and kitchen downstairs and upstairs they've got another lounge and beds. Sometimes we sit on the bus a lot instead of hanging out in dressing rooms at venues before a show, because we can play Xbox or listen to music.

This big American TV channel came and filmed on our tour bus once in the US for a behind-the-scenes show, and Connor and I had left our protein shake bottles in the cupboard for a couple of weeks with milk still inside and they curdled. It was the most disgusting thing I've ever smelt in my life. When they opened the cupboard, Tris smelt it and nearly threw up. They caught it all on video and it's so funny.

TRISTAN: I still remember that smell now. It was indescribably bad. It's like I'll never be able to get it out of my nose.

We don't mind sharing space with each other on the bus. None of us went to uni but I imagine it's a bit like living in a student house. You're with a load of mates very tightly packed in having a laugh.

The bunk beds are actually really comfortable. They're like a cocoon and the sound of the bus engine kind of lulls you to sleep.

**CON:** The tour bus is such a laugh because we can play *FIFA* and sleep, but this one time our bus broke down in America really early on in the tour and that was hideous. It happened on Fin's birthday as well.

As Brad said, we couldn't get another one so we ended up having to fly everywhere and sleep in hotels instead just getting into our bunks each night. We'd wake up, say hi to fans at the airport, get on a plane, do a gig and then go to sleep again. We were so tired. That was the worst touring experience we've had.

Although it was also pretty awful when I tried to get into a bunk with our in-ears guy, Ben, once. I'd been out and I clambered back onto the bus and tried to get into his bunk, thinking it was mine. He was fast asleep. I think I must have finally realised, so in the end I gave up and fell asleep in the aisle. Poor Fin had to lift me into my bunk.

**JAMES:** We all sleep on the tour bus quite a lot. I often grab an hour before we go on stage on tour because it relaxes me. The good thing now is that we know each other so well we don't have to be polite and it's not like we have to spend all our time together. We can have time to ourselves in our bunks if we want a break.

I really like the tour bus generally but I hate not being able to shower in the morning. And you also can't poo on the bus. It's a rule. Tristan did it once and he got in so much trouble with Fin.

If we don't need to do a long overnight journey we nearly always get to stay in quite nice hotels, but back in the early days some of the places we stayed in were pretty awful. We stayed in one in London where the window was hanging off its hinges and there was an old mattress in the room.

**CON:** The worst one ever was after a summer show in Wales, and it still gives me nightmares. We didn't have a hotel to stay in because everywhere was booked up so we ended up going to this holiday camp in the middle of a field.

When we arrived the first thing they said to us was, 'Have you got your own bed sheets?' When we said no they gave us some that were like cardboard.

We went for a wander around and walked into this random bar where there was a disco going on. Everyone stared at us and then this young guy shouted, 'Look, it's Two Direction.' Then a group of lads came over and told us we had to leave because they didn't like us. It was so weird. We're not exactly the fighting type so we just sloped back to our rooms.

Tristan and I were sharing a room and when we opened the door there was a bucket and spade on the floor that had been left by the previous guests. There were also a pair of dirty children's shoes by the window, a wet duvet in the wardrobe, and kiss marks on the mirror on the bathroom. Oh yes, and we mustn't forget the used razors and wee on the bathroom floor.

Tristan woke up in the middle of the night and started saying there was someone in the wardrobe. He was having night horrors because the place was so awful. He was convinced there was someone else in the room. It was honestly the worst place I've ever stayed in and I'm still scarred by it.

**JAMES:** There was a guy asleep outside Joe and Dean's bedroom. He'd literally just passed out on the pavement with a can of beer still in his hand. We were so happy to leave the following morning.

**CON:** Some guys started on Tris and me when we were staying in a hotel in Wales another time. There was a wedding in the main bar and Tris and I went to have a look at what was going on. All of a sudden this guy came out, pushed us against a wall and threatened to punch us! He followed us down the stairs and when he saw our crew he started on them too. He was smashed out of his face.

**TRISTAN:** We have had some weird experiences on the road, but it's never boring and we always come back with some good stories.

**CON:** How nice your dressing room is totally depends on where you are. The ones at the O2 are pretty good, but sometimes they're pretty grim. I think people assume they're going to have candles and massive comfy sofas in them, but sadly not.

People are always disappointed when they ask about our rider too. They expect it to be full of Jack Daniel's and caviar but we would find it embarrassing if we asked for ridiculous things. The craziest thing we get is probably ginger, which is for Brad to drink with honey in some hot water to soothe his throat.

We have drinks and fruit and crisps but Fin doesn't let us have any alcohol. We can always have a drink afterwards if we want to.

**BRAD:** We also have a big backstage box that's full of things like weights, Frisbees and footballs. It's like a teenage boy's box.

I came up with the idea to have a cocktail-making box as well so we could have a different themed cocktail for every night we toured, but that got shot down by Fin pretty quickly. I still think it's a great idea. And I could learn to make cocktails. Win win!

**JAMES:** We're quite chilled out backstage. We might play table tennis or football, but other than that Brad will do vocal warm-ups, I'll do weights sometimes, and we'll mess around making up games or challenges. We always feel like we've got tons of time before a show and then Fin will suddenly say, 'You've got ten minutes!' and we'll run around panicking.

I'm usually more energetic earlier in the day because I wake up early and I go to bed early. I find it hard to retain energy between the time we eat at 6 p.m. and then go on stage at 9 p.m., so I like to have a good half an hour to build myself up to performing. The other boys' dream work day would start at 3 p.m. and go on until 4 a.m., but I prefer having nine to five hours, so I find late shows quite hard sometimes.

**CON:** Our Wizzboards are so much fun, and genuinely helpful for me. I was using mine a lot at home to get around when my knee was bad.

I used it on stage on the last tour too and that made some people quite nervous because they thought I was going to zoom off the end of the stage. But I've fallen off stage without it so it would be no different.

**TRISTAN:** One thing we always do just before we go on stage is rub our chins together. It's a luck thing. We started doing it at the beginning of The Vamps and I don't know how or why.

How many seconds we do it for depends on the date. So if it's, say, 31 January, we have to do it for thirty-one seconds. It starts to hurt after about twenty seconds and I get bored.

**BRAD:** We've never played a show without rubbing our chins together. I remember when I went down with tonsillitis the first time

we went to Australia. I was so ill I had to stay in Sydney and the guys went to Brisbane and played a show without me. They'd never done that before so they Facetimed me as they rubbed their chins together.

It was weird when Con was out of action with his knee injury. It didn't ever feel right not having him so we Facetimed him before shows and did the chin thing.

**CON:** Seeing the lads doing everything without me was such a horrible feeling. I'd look at their pictures on Twitter and Instagram and see them having fun and I felt sad I wasn't with them.

And then I saw a picture that devastated me – they'd replaced me with Prince Charles. They were all at the Prince's Trust Celebrate Success Awards laughing and joking. How was I supposed to compete with that?

**BRAD:** I totally get that because there was a period towards the end of last year when I had some trouble with my voice and I had to come back early from America, and I hated not being with the other guys.

I went to see a doctor and he said I had to fly home straight away because I had acid reflux, which meant that when I ate the acid came back up. It's probably the worst thing a singer can have because it means there's acid sitting on your vocal folds.

I'd always been lucky I had no problems with my voice so that really shook me. I had three weeks off but I started recovering properly after two. I didn't speak for that whole time so my throat could heal and it was *so* hard. It drove me mad not being with the rest of the band while they were cracking on.

**JAMES:** We also do a little speech if we do a headline show, which has kind of escalated over time. I saw Taylor Swift doing it with her crew on a documentary and it was such a nice thing to do.

We've taken it to a level and now everyone has to hold an item when they do it. It started off being a fork or something, but now we grab tables and chairs, and I even picked up Blake from New Hope Club once. It's become like a competition to find the best item you can in the dressing room.

**BRAD:** It's weird because you can be feeling so rubbish before you go on stage if you're ill, and then all of a sudden you feel fine once you're on there. We call it Doctor Stage because it seems to cure all ills. You may feel awful when you get off, but while you're doing the performance you're OK.

**TRISTAN:** We can see a lot of people from the stage. I think people assume we can't see all the way to the back, and maybe we can't at venues like the O2 where it's really high in places, but we can see a lot. The only time when we can't see out is when the spotlight is on us because we're a bit blinded.

We can see the audience so clearly Brad has picked people out before if they're not standing up, and we can spot our friends and family.

We don't have a wind-down ritual in the dressing room after we leave stage because we're usually out of a venue and on the bus within sixty seconds. If it's an event where there's another act we want to watch we'll stay on, but otherwise we usually have to get out pretty quickly.

We'll sometimes have a couple of drinks in the hotel bar after a show. It's nice to hang out with the other guys because you come off stage on such a high and it can feel quite flat if you're just in a hotel room on your own. It's hard to comprehend what you've just done but it feels amazing.

I can see how people end up turning to drugs when they tour a lot because they're chasing that high. But I've never touched a drug in my life and I'm really proud of that. It's not a road I would ever go down. Some of my idols, like Steven Tyler, have had problems with drugs, and hearing them talk about why they did them I can almost understand it. But we've all got our heads screwed on too well.

My dad gave me two bits of advice when I was young: don't ride a motorbike, and don't do drugs because they'll ruin your life – and they've always stuck with me. Those are two good rules to live your life by.

**BRAD:** It feels weird when you come off stage because you're still buzzing, but even sitting and having a chat to each other on the bus afterwards helps.

We always know whether a show's been good or not. A good show for us is when the fans have interacted. We love it when we see them clapping and jumping up and down when we are. If the crowd is receptive it really lifts us.

You get out what you put into a show, and if we're going a bit mad then generally the crowd will do the same, so it's up to us to generate that excitement.

**CON:** Obviously I've fallen over on stage the most times out of all of us, but Brad is the one who slips sometimes because he's always running around and jumping on things while he's performing.

James and Tristan have never fallen over (let's be honest, it's harder for Tristan to fall over), but Brad and James ran into each other when we were supporting McBusted at Hyde Park. Brad didn't see James and he turned around really quickly and whacked into him and popped his nose. It was bleeding pretty badly but Brad still managed to finish the song.

**BRAD:** I went straight to A&E when I got off stage and I waited four hours to be seen. I managed to get back to the bar just as McBusted finished their set so I did pretty well though.

**JAMES:** I've never had an injury caused by being on stage, but I did have quite a bad one because of my guitar. When we did our first arena tour in April 2015, without realising I had my guitar an inch lower on my strap than I usually do; I woke up two days after the tour finished with a horrible pain in my wrist.

I had no idea what was causing it and thought it would go after a few days. I Googled the symptoms and it sounded like I had repetitive strain, so I skipped the gym for a couple of weeks thinking it would get better on its own.

A few months on it was still painful and by the end of the year it was still as sore. I was really worried because playing guitar is my job, so I ended up going to hospital to have a scan. When he looked at the scan results the doctor said it was one of the worst wrist tendon injuries he'd ever seen.

I ended up having wrist surgery over Christmas and my arm was in a sling for months. It took a year to properly repair, and it's really only recently the pain has completely gone. It meant I wasn't able to play a lot of guitar on the second album, which I was gutted about.

**BRAD:** We don't go too crazy with partying when we're on tour because you can get really run down if you're doing a show every night and we want to be on top form. We tend to have family drinks at the London show and then a crew night out at the end of the tour, and then some nights in between. But we know our limits.

**JAMES:** Well, I do! I've never been hungover on stage, incredibly.

The other lads will go out after the show sometimes but I've never been into clubbing, and I took a whole year off drinking last year. I drank on New Year's Eve 2014 and then I didn't drink for a couple of weeks. That turned into a few months, and by the time I reached six months I thought I might as well do the whole year.

Drinking, going out and loud music isn't really my thing. When I was younger and my mates were going out and getting drunk I preferred staying in and watching *The Bill* or *Coronation Street*. People may think that's strange but it's what I enjoyed doing.

**CON:** There have been times when Tris, Brad and I have had a few too many drinks the night before a show, and we've always regretted it so we don't do it any more. The thing is, if we're feeling rough we've just got to get on with it. We can't phone in sick to work if we've got a show to do, but it feels horrible if you sing when you're not 100 per cent.

**BRAD:** When we toured with McFly I did quite a lot of partying. Because we were the support we only played four songs so I could get away with it. But now we do sets that last for an hour and a half and they really take their toll on your voice and your body.

There's no way I can have a big night in the middle of the tour because it makes the show the next night not as good. Then that has a knock-on effect on the rest of the shows because you don't get a chance to catch up. Now I only go out at the end of the tour, or if we don't have a show the following day.

I'll never forget when Con and I went out after a gig a couple of years ago. We got in at 6 a.m. and I was definitely still drunk when I woke up. I started to feel terrible at around 5 p.m and we were performing that night. I was so close to being sick during the show.

When I left the stage I thought I was going to collapse. That was one of those times where Doctor Stage does *not* cure everything. Ever since then I've learnt my lesson, especially as I seem to suffer more as I get older. Tristan's hangovers are worse too, but I reckon that's because he drinks champagne. And far too much of it.

**JAMES:** I'm always the one who's a bit negative and reminds everyone that we have to work the following day. Usually I'll be in bed by midnight, while the others will be trying to find somewhere else to go on to and party more.

Although I'm not big on going out there are some things I really enjoy going to. I like going to events like London Fashion Week, and the BRITs after-party was really good this year.

I like to be in control and I'm not very good at letting go, but I did at the BRITs do. I got to bed at 5.30 a.m. and I really enjoyed myself. You meet so many good people through those kinds of events.

**TRISTAN:** The BRITs after-party was a big one for us. Justin Bieber was there and we joined Louis from One Direction's table. I've got such good memories of it but we got smashed. Brad foolishly went to the gym with James the following morning thinking it would make him feel better and he just sat there and watched while James did a workout.

**BRAD:** I lifted one weight and then went to the sauna.

**CON:** I think we have the best nights out when it's all four of us, but Tris and I go out most. I prefer going to student nights rather than posh clubs because I hate that whole scene. I would much rather go to smaller venues where everyone's up for having a good time.

I got papped coming out of a nightclub once, and I never want that to happen again because I was mortified. It was all free drink at the party and I'd gone a bit crazy after the excitement of the show. I was doing Jägerbombs and tequila and all sorts, and I was so gone James and Tristan had to carry me out.

We were performing the following day and I felt the worst I'd *ever* felt in my life. I was flicking through my phone during rehearsals and I saw that the main picture on the *Sun*'s showbiz page was me looking horrendous. I was so drunk I hadn't even noticed the paps. I felt awful for about a week.

**BRAD:** We went out in Cardiff one night and we got given free drinks in this bar. We got quite drunk and we took over the dance floor. We all like having a bit of a dance after a few drinks but we're not that *great*.

We were dancing away and all of a sudden Fin ripped his shirt open. At that point the bar manager walked up to our security and asked who was in charge. They all pointed at Fin, who at that point was on the dance floor partying with the rest of us. I don't think the manager was that impressed.

Sometimes we have to be a bit careful when we're out because guys think it's clever to be able to tell their mates that they started on one of The Vamps. We were in a club a while back and we were talking to some girls. This group of lads really didn't like it and one of them came over to me, grabbed my hat off my head and threw it across the room.

You never know what to do in that situation but considering he was about four foot taller than me I thought it was best to do nothing. We didn't have security or anything with us so I wasn't about to argue with him. I just went and got my hat, had another drink and let him get on with being an idiot.

**CON:** The guy was much older than us because we were probably only about eighteen at the time, and he thought he was being so clever. The thing is, we don't want to have to take security out with us all the time. I guess we're safer when we have it, but we don't like it. We'd much rather be on our own.

If we want to properly relax it's better to have security, even if they don't make it obvious they are there, because then we don't have to worry and we can enjoy our night.

We don't get a lot of hassle and most guys are really fine with us, but you do get the odd one who thinks he's cool. But then I'll get on the dance floor and he'll realise he's not.

WHERE WE ARE NOW

FRIENDSHIPS, FAME AND THE
ONE THING TRISTAN WILL
NEVER FORGIVE JAMES FOR

**JAMES:** The dynamic in the band has kind of changed from when we first started out. I guess because I was the first member of the band and the eldest I was a bit of a dad figure.

Brad was younger than me so I took on a bit of a parental role with him when we met, and even though Tristan was older than me when he joined the band it was kind of the same with him. When Connor came along he was still quite young so I guess I stayed in that role for a while. But now it's really even and equal between us all.

We've all still got roles to a certain extent, though. If the record label or management need something posted on Twitter or a phone interview done they'll ask me to do it because they know I will!

On the other end of the spectrum, Tristan is really good at the socialising and networking, which is great. I find it hard to speak to people I don't know, whereas Tristan can talk to anyone and he'll go up to random people and start chatting.

Brad is kind of in between Tris and me because he can be sensible at times but he likes going out and he's great at building relationships with people. Connor is more like me because he can still be shy, but he can also be very chatty after a few drinks.

At the end of the day, we've all got the same goals, and that's to take the band as far as we possibly can. We all work together to achieve everything we want to, and we complement each other.

**TRISTAN:** We all get on really well and we never argue In the band in a petty way because if we're annoyed about something we'll just tell each other. And we're always debating so that gets everything out. We're pretty grown up in that way. We'll get it all out in the open and then it's forgotten an hour later.

Sometimes James is so focused I think he needs to relax more, and maybe I'm a little too laidback at times. I'm also messy as hell, and so are Connor and Brad, and it drives James mad if the tour bus is a mess.

We'll get annoyed when James wants to go to bed really early because we want to hang out with him, but that's literally the only negative thing you can say about him.

We're best friends, and thank God because it would be hell if we weren't. Sometimes we spend twenty-four hours a day together and we never get bored or annoyed by each other's company. We bug each other about stupid normal stuff and it could be so much worse considering we're rarely apart.

We all know our place and we give everyone their freedom to do their own thing. I'm not the singer, I'm the drummer. I'm the producer, not the writer. We have so much respect for each other.

**JAMES:** I don't think Connor has ever been involved in any kind of argument we've had because he's so laidback. He's a real pacifist and he'll just sit there and chill while it all goes on around him.

If we do fall out it'll be over stupid things like if someone is late, but it's nice that we let it go really quickly. And it's never personal; it's more about a situation.

Sometimes when we've been on tour for a long time we can get a bit agitated and we're ready to go home and have our own space, so we can get frustrated over little things. But we know each other so well now and we know what will wind each other up so we're respectful and we make sure we don't do those things.

**BRAD:** We've all got different relationships with each other, but it's kind of a level playing field. We're all very chilled out and there are no egos getting in the way. We never have to suck up to anyone to keep them happy. We've all got respect for each other and everyone around us.

**TRISTAN:** We would never try to act like we were something special. All the people around us keep us down to earth, and we also keep each other down to earth. We're not the kind of guys who want to be friends with people just because they're well known.

**CON:** A lot of famous people ditch their friends and become mates with famous people instead when they get a bit of success. That changes you as a person because the people you're around influence you. We don't *want* to change. Sometimes people just want to be mates with you to climb the ladder, but the people you've known for a long time haven't got an ulterior motive.

**JAMES:** Some people I knew at school have tried to latch on and be friends since the band took off and that sucks. It's always so obvious. And there are people we've met in the industry who have either ignored us or been quite rude, and then a couple of years down the line now we're successful they're being really nice.

We like sincerity in the band, but some people are a product of the industry and they'll be talking to you while looking over your shoulder in case someone cooler comes along.

**CON:** Every industry is the same really, and everyone does that to a certain extent in their job. It's horrible but at least we have the other 'normal' side of our lives as well, so we have a good balance.

Some of the nicest people we've met are the most famous, like Taylor Swift and Ed Sheeran. It's people who have just come into the industry that want to use *people* instead of *talent* to get to where they want to be that you have to be wary of.

**BRAD:** To be fair I did expect the music industry to be a bit dog eat dog anyway, because no one is ever happy at the level they're at. Everyone's always looking to do better and some people will use you to elevate themselves.

It's quite hard meeting girls for the same reason. You really don't know who you can and can't trust. It's horrible when you trust someone and they let you down. It opens your eyes a bit and now we spot it a bit earlier and we're not as naive.

**JAMES:** I think we're all pretty good at recognising people who are chasing us because of who we are. If we go out to a club and girls are around us we would never take advantage just because we could, and we take it all with a pinch of salt.

I've dated a couple of girls and I've known pretty much from the start that it was superficial. We're used to girls liking us for *who* we are not *what* we are because we had girlfriends before we were in the band, but we've met a lot of girls along the way who have been all over us one minute, and onto someone else the next.

**TRISTAN:** We don't feel like we have to surround ourselves with loads of people to impress anyone or have a massive entourage either. We're very well sheltered from the crap and Richard is amazing at keeping us grounded. His track record is incredible and we've had nothing but positive comments from other people he's worked with.

I'm very happy to listen to our managers' advice and follow their instructions if we have to be somewhere at a certain time or do something for work. But I must admit I'm not very good at being told something when I think I know better. Although it's rare that I do know better. I've always been very headstrong.

All of our parents get along really well and it's so nice having them around a lot. I think that also stops us getting carried away with things.

I love the fact I've made my mum and dad proud of me. My dad is really into music so to be able to take him backstage at the O2 is incredible. I'm also doing OK financially and I feel like I've taken some worry off their shoulders because they know I'm well looked after in the band.

**JAMES:** It's so weird when people use the word 'famous' when they talk about us because we really don't feel like we are. When we're playing massive venues like the O2 we think, 'This is amazing,' but it's not like, 'Wow, we're awesome.' It's just appreciation.

We find the whole fame thing funny and we laugh when we see people act like celebrities. It's really alien to us. We really enjoy the fact we're not affected by it all. No one is better than anyone else, no matter what job they do.

I think when I knew we were 'known' was when 'Can We Dance' went to number two in the charts, and then we sold out our first tour. We were having breakfast in LA when we found out. The tickets had been on sale while we'd been sleeping and it was incomprehensible to me because I had no idea if we'd sell *any* tickets, let alone sell them *all*.

Things like selling out the O2 twice, releasing a second album and going on big TV shows are proper realisation moments.

**CON:** We're level-headed about everything though. Ultimately 'fame' is flash in the pan. It's always got a sell-by date and music doesn't always last.

You have to actively be famous to be a celebrity and you're portraying an image that isn't real, and that's not us. Some people turn up at events and act like they're so much more important than everyone else and they won't speak to people and they expect really over-the-top treatment.

We do get the fact you've got to play the game sometimes, and there are some days where you have to slap on a smile even if you're feeling crap. But everyone is a bit different when they're at work. You wouldn't go into an office job and act the same as you would with your family or friends.

**BRAD:** The first couple of years we were in the industry we were a bit like deer caught in the headlights, but now we know how it all works. We've done two arena tours so we know we're doing pretty OK, but we're still not part of the superficial side of it. We hear stories about how other artists act and we're always shocked. As Tris said, the fact we've got our families around us and we've still got the same friends we've always had makes a massive difference.

**JAMES:** We're also very aware that not everyone is going to like us, and don't expect them to.

The situation with Fifth Harmony was the first time we experienced proper hate online, and we all really supported each other through that. I could understand it if we'd intentionally set out to hurt someone, but we honestly hadn't.

It was a really hard time for Brad. He'd been trying to keep a relationship going from thousands of miles away and he hadn't seen Lauren for ages. She was a girl he really liked but both of their schedules were so busy they didn't have time to see each other. It got to a point where the relationship was taking place over the phone and it was destroying Brad because he wanted to be with her.

He tried his best to deal with it in the right way possible, and when the relationship ended it was hard for both of them. He wanted to try and get on with his life but he was asked about Lauren constantly and he'd have to try and explain it over and over again. It was very raw for him and we saw how badly he was affected.

What we said was totally taken out of context and we were labelled sexist. Yes, in retrospect, we were disrespectful to talk about the situation in that way and we hold our hands up to that, but we were honestly just trying to use humour to deflect attention away from Brad.

Usually if we finish an interview and we've said something wrong we know straight away, but we ended that interview thinking it was fine and it had gone well. It wasn't until we woke up the following morning that we realised that people had taken the words we said, twisted them and gone crazy.

I texted Lauren and apologised straight away and she was fine about it. As far as The Vamps and Fifth Harmony were concerned it was all cool, but other people made it a big deal.

The boys have done the same for me before when I've been asked difficult questions. I was dating Sophie Turner from *Game of Thrones* for a while and they used to help me out when I was asked about her all the time. It's just what we do. We've got each other's backs.

I do hope people think we're nice because we really are. I guess what's happened made us more conscious of what we say and how easily a joke can be taken out of context. It was a massive reality check for us because we'd never had to deal with anything like that before.

Even now, two years later, people make comments about Fifth Harmony to us online. But I guess that's social media for you. It will probably always happen in some way.

**BRAD:** I know it sounds crazy but if I wasn't in the band I wouldn't have any social media at all. Zero. And it would be the best thing ever. I spoke to a lad the other day who only has Snapchat – no Twitter or Facebook – and that's the dream. I say that and then I'd probably get bored and gravitate back to it eventually.

**JAMES:** I've had to delete some things on Twitter in the past. To be fair I do probably tweet five times as much as the other boys so it's bound to happen sometimes.

I've replied to hate when I shouldn't have done. I know I shouldn't but I find it frustrating. All we can do is to try and detach ourselves. I've realised there's no point in replying to negative comments.

Social media isn't just what got us started; it's what has kept us going, and we are very grateful for that.

**BRAD:** We're in an incredible position but sometimes it can be hard. Social media can make you very anxious because you're constantly under the microscope. Because of that you can start overanalysing everything and it makes you think too much. I've got a friend who suffers from terrible anxiety and I think a lot of people struggle with it but often don't speak about it. My struggle is no worse than his just because people know who I am and are writing nasty things about me on Twitter.

I remember telling my mate I was having a hard time once and he was so shocked because he didn't expect me to get affected by things. But we're not invincible; we're normal lads and we don't get to go home and talk to our parents and friends every night. We don't take anything for granted, but it's not all glamour and fun.

**JAMES:** It's been difficult having relationships now we're in the public eye. At the start of the band, Brad and I were both in long-term relationships. I was with my first-ever girlfriend and we'd been together for four years, but due to the band there just wasn't time for us to be together. We struggled for the last year of the relationship and then ultimately it ended.

Maintaining relationships is really difficult and it's hard for a girlfriend to see us go on tour and get pictured with other girls and hear rumours about what we're doing, even though they're not true.

I've been linked with so many people since the band started. I had a photo taken with Kendall Jenner at a party once and people started saying we were dating. I put a picture up on Twitter of me with my sister and people even started claiming I was dating a 'mystery girl'!

When I dated Sophie Turner it was difficult to keep it under wraps because we were pictured by fans outside hotels a few times and it was quite obvious something was going on. I think because we were both in the public eye there was quite a lot of pressure on us and it felt like everything was on fast forward because everyone was speculating about us.

People I've dated have had a really hard time on Twitter so I think it's easier to keep that side of my life private now. I'm not keeping secrets, I'm probably just not as open as I used to be.

BRAD: Sometimes when things are hard you need the support of your friends and family. And if ever we get down about anything we can talk to each other. There are times when the only people who can really relate to what we're going through are the other three band members because they're probably going through the same thing.

If a problem is something to do with the band we're probably the best people to speak to, but you also need that older, wiser figure to give you some perspective on things sometimes. And sometimes you just want to pick up the phone to your mum.

JAMES: The great thing about being in the band is that everything was new for all of us and we're experiencing it together. It's nice to be able to share the experiences and the things that go with it.

Fame and being known around the world is quite intense and intimidating at times. It can be quite hard to deal with and we share all of that. If there's anything we're unsure or nervous about we've always got each other, and that makes it so much easier.

CON: Brad and I had a night out in Milan after a show once and we were having a really deep conversation in a bar. Suddenly we both started bawling our eyes out. We were crying on each other's shoulders like nine-year-olds. Everyone in the club must have been staring at us like we were insane. But sometimes you need to do that to get it all out and talk about things. We both felt better, if a bit worse for wear, the next day.

**JAMES:** At the end of the day, music is why we started the band, and while we know all of the other stuff comes with it, that's what we focus on.

We all have a passion for music and come from musical backgrounds so we all contribute to that side of things. The other guys are into producing so a lot of the time we'll ask each other's opinions and we collaborate all the time.

**BRAD:** I've got a studio at home so I recorded quite a lot of the second and third album there. The tracks were only in demo form so we then took them into a big studio and recorded them properly. Con and Tristan do the same, and it means we can try stuff out first to see what works best.

In the beginning we used to have to stick to acoustic guitar-type music and if we got stuck we'd work with other people, but now we can create songs completely ourselves. Because we write and produce our own music we don't have to wait for people to send us songs; we can just crack on when we want to.

**CON:** We love being in the studio recording new music because it's so chilled and we can be really creative. Quite often Brad is in the vocal booth for quite a long time and the rest of us get to relax, play games and write. And we eat a lot of pizza.

When we're making new music we're always influenced by what's around us in the world, whether that's music or trends. We've travelled the world now so we've got a lot more to write about than we did a few years ago.

**BRAD:** We had a lot of time to work on the first album, *Meet The Vamps*, so I don't think we were consciously working on a sound. There was a lot of folk music around at that time which influenced us so it was very acoustic, guitar-driven and quite upbeat and feel-good.

With the second album, *Wake Up*, we'd toured more and developed more of a sound as a live band. And although we were really happy with *Wake Up*, we felt like we missed a bit of the youthful fun of *Meet The Vamps* in a way, so we're planning to bring that back for the third album.

That's everything from us for now. We really hope you enjoyed the book. We had such a laugh writing it and reflecting back on all the mad things that have happened to us so far. And we're looking forward to plenty more happening in the future.

We want to take this opportunity to say a thank you to all of you. It's because of you The Vamps exist, and we're four mates having the time of our lives. We couldn't have done any of it without your support.

We love you!

BRAD, JAMES, CON AND TRIS XX

Abbey Simmons, Abbie Cunningham, Abbie Green, Abbie Harding, Abbie Hodgkins, Abbie Kipps, Abbie Sussex, Abby Charlton, Abigail Gore, Abigail JC, Abigail Shields, Abigail Woolhouse, Adriane Cernal, Adrianna Śmiałek, Aina Mae Kirsten B. Reyes, Alannah Thompson, Alba Saunders, Alessandro Zoccarato, Alessandro Paini, Alessia Formolo, Alexandra Deloge, Alexandra Potter Villafane, Alice Allen, Alice Murphy, Alice Stones, Alice Penegar, Alicia Goodwin, Alicia Jackson, Aline Zavala, Alisha Johnson, Alix Daverson, Alysha Marment, Alyssa Andrews, Amanda Randonis, Amani Mughal, Amber Pallett, Amber Kassa Thomson, Amber Leigh Amos, Ambi Leia , Amelia Nielsen, Ami Brewis, Amie Boswell, Amie Humphrey, Amy Carr, Amy Garvie, Amy Hadridge, Amy Kirkop, Amy McQuaid, Amy Rutherford, Amy Waller, Amy Whitehead, Amy Williams, Amy Asano Campbell, Amy Jessica Grant, Ana Puebla, Ana Carolina Melo, Anais Liger, Anaïs Da Silva Matos, Andrew , Angelika Lipska, Anke Van Bylen, Anna Alho, Anna Fichtner, Anna Rékó, Annabel Prowen, Annabel Rogers, Annabelle Craven, Annaise Ramkalawan, Anne Austin, Annika Koivistoinen, Annika Lehtomaki, Antonia Turmaine, Anusha Butt, Anya Niamh Jones, Ariane Reichardt, Aricka Alexander, Ashleigh Pike, Ashleigh Latter, Ashley Campbell, Ashley Jones, Atsuko Koide, Aurélie Vasseur, Ava Alesbury, Ava Frohock, Ava Lawrence, Barbara Allison, Barbara Lemos, Barry Maye, Beatrice Bleakley, Becky Ayers, Becky Hartminck, Becky Jane, Becky Murray, Bella Poland, Ben Aldridge, Beth Dalrymple, Beth Hodges, Beth and Molly Summers, Bethan Phillips, Bethanie Hurst, Bethany Caine, Bethany Dunford, Bethany Miller, Bethany Rosevear, Bethany Stanford, Bethany Arrand, Bethany Heath, Bethany Johnson, Bethany Strange, Bethany Louise Chaplin, Bianca Kwan, Bianca Moiteiro, Bianca Sauter, Blaise de Castro, Blanca Fernández, Blue-Rosetter Trench, Bobbie Jade Solkhon, Bobbie-Louise Booth, Brechtje Oliedam, Brian McCafferty, Brianda Lubel, Britney Ross, Brooke Hamilton, Bry Hopley, Bryony Neville, Caitlin Bromley, Caitlin Chun, Caitlin Garty, Caitlin Jordan, Caitlin Miller, Caitlin Reaves, Caitlin Rogers, Caitlin Thorburn, Caitlin Gallacher, Caitlin Evans, Caitlin Lara Whitelely, Caitlyn Talbot, Caleigh Capek, Caleigh Noelle, Camila Lisanti, Camilla Stangalino, Camille Dick, Candice Eales, Cara Nicholl, Carolina Ferraz, Carolina Tanaka, Caroline Roberts, Carys Boxell, Cassie Senn, Catherine Southgate, Cerys Armitage, Charlene del Valle, Charley Coleman, Charley-Jo Bell, Charlotte Beagley, Charlotte Biggs, Charlotte Dickinson, Charlotte Martin, Charlotte Mayes, Charlotte Mills, Charlotte Walton, Charlotte Welch, Charlotte Daue, Charmaine Chan, Chelsea Allison, Chelsea Berry, Chelsea Jones, Chelsea Leonard, Chelsea Rutherford, Chelsea Woolley, Chiara Pitino, Chloe Bruce, Chloe Clarke, Chloe Clarke, Chloe Cooper, Chloe Davenport, Chloe Foster, Chloe Green, Chloe Grime, Chloe Hume, Chloe Ludkin, Chloe McKenna, Chloe Watkins, Chloë Miller, Chloë Janssens, Chloé Bruhl, Chloé Legrand, Chloe Ann Foster, Christine Nely, Cielo Eunice, Claire Baker, Claire Roberts, Claire Williams, Claire Hannah Cavanagh, Clarisa Scattareggia, Clodagh Rush, Connie Neaves, Connie Stephens, Coralie Lorge, Courtney Morris, Courtney Sibley, Daisy Fletcher, Daisy Turner, Daisy-May Worsell, Danae Charala, Dani Ramsden, Daniel Mazz, Daniel Baynham, Daniela Hyslop, Danielle Beaumont, Danielle Beck, Danielle Jordan, Danielle Melody, Danielle Meyer, Danielle Stack, Danni Merrell, Darcey Dorothy Blane, Debbie Akomanyi, Deborah Magee, Delphine Horler, Demy Jongepier, Deryn Edwards, Ebba Johansson Magnusson, Eilish Cunningham, Elaine Denton, Elan Duggan, Eleanor Ambekar, Eleanor Freeman, Eleanor Gouldie, Elena Aubà, Eleri Beth Williams, Elettra North Finocchi, Eli Gabrielle Jamnasingh, Elisa Daniele, Elisa Pinheiro, Elise Tonks, Elisha Corfield, Elisha Nicholls, Elizabeth Aworetan, Elizabeth Schwartz, Ella Tucker, Ellen Girling, Ellen Jones, Ellie Amelia, Ellie Corney, Ellie Graham, Ellie Jenkins, Ellie Lunnenkay, Ellie White, Elliot Whyte, Elsa Legarlantezeck, Elysa Dimitrakis, Em Adams, Emilie Jones, Emily Beth, Emily Blake, Emily Day, Emily Duckett, Emily Emerson, Emily Gridley, Emily Hatfield, Emily Jenkins, Emily King, Emily Lofts, Emily Mann, Emily Morgan, Emily Parker, Emily Quaid Dunn, Emily Strickland, Emily Williams, Emily Ann Dunn, Emily Grace Wragg, Emily Jane Wheeler, Emily Lauren Hills, Emily-Jo McGrath-Gray, Emma Briedis, Emma Dee, Emma Donegan, Emma Hayward, Emma Hurley, Emma Lecuir, Emma Lee, Emma Mathews, Emma McKendrick, Emma Miller, Emma Okoli, Emma Oliver, Emma Sidaway, Emma Söderström, Emma Straghan, Emma Thomson, Emma Thornton, Emma Wallskog, Emma Ward, Emma Watts, Emma Wilson, Emma Wyke, Emma Louise Shaw, Emmie Watson, Emmy Clifford, Eponine Montaigu, Erin Green, Erin Houston, Erin McCullough, Erin Walls, Esther Swain, Esther Wong, Eva Aires, Eve Henley, Evie Mullen, Farah Sheikh, Faye AlMulla, Faye Maddocks, Fien Volkaerts, Fiona Summers, Fionnuala McCallum, Fizza Parsayan, Flo Nikkessen, Florence Juhel, Francesca Carrieri, Francesca Cusack, Francesca Trazza, Frankie Townsend, Freya Atherton, Gabby Coughlan, Gabby Dodd, Gabrielle Trasporto, Gaby Lloyd, Gaby Lugue, Gemma Carey, Gemma Menzies, Georgia Galbraith, Georgia Hewitt, Georgia Reaves, Georgia Willerton, Georgia Edward, Georgia Ledbury, Georgia Price, Georgia Louise De Lima, Georgie Tyms, Georgina Barratt, Georgina Dawson, Georgina Eales, Georgina Sockett, Gigi , Gio Edards, Giovanna Manfré, Giuliana Leonelli, Grace Cooney, Grace Lord, Grace Mason, Greta Larosa, Gweneira van Koot, Hanan Eisele, Hanisi Ingram, Hanna Jauhiainen, Hannah Bonnie, Hannah Gatenby, Hannah Manning, Hannah McLean, Hannah Ormandy, Hannah Patrick, Hannah Rodgers, Hannah Simpson, Hannah Singleton, Hannah Sloper, Hannah Starkey, Hannah Thomas, Hannah Kirkwood, Harley Rowen, Harley Wilcoxson, Harriet Aburn, Harriet Lea-Brammer, Harriet Loveridge, Heather Caine, Heather Causer, Heidi Dixon, Heike Schoger, Helen Bauer, Hilde Marie Welle, Hoda H. Ezzat, Hollie Acreman, Hollie Creasy, Holly Ashley, Holly Bale, Holly Clark, Holly Dillon, Holly Findlay, Holly Finerty, Holly Hunter, Holly Meehan, Holly Parr, Holly Swain, Holly Yu, Hope-Leigh Baldwin, Hugo Gómez, Ifa Hanifaputri, Ignacia Marambio, India Chilvers, Inês Pereira, Iniki Fazzina, Isa Ackroyd, Isabel Lithgow, Isabela Rena, Isabella Deacon, Isabella Knapp, Isabella Poderico, Isabelle Kate Walker, Ishi Malhotra, Ishita Sharma, Isobel Duke, Isobel Winward-Jones, Iva Pejic, Izzie C, Jackii Robles Ch., Jade Brandon, Jade Cooper, Jade Jones, Jade Pilbro, Jade Pugh, Jade Spencer, Jade Ward, Jamie-Lee Wynne, Janeo Tan, Janine Cameron, Jasmin Carranza, Jasmine Baguio, Jasmine del Castillo Bondoc, Jasmine Fidler, Jasmine Yaqub, Jasmine Alice King, Javiera Monardes González, Jay Styler, Jazmin Price, Jemima Gorst, Jemma Clark, Jemma Corriea, Jenna Gourlay, Jennie Beale, Jennifer Louise Bedson, Jenny Long, Jeorjah McEwen, Jeska Kelly, Jess Castledine, Jess Davis, Jess Friend, Jess Oatham, Jess Wingrove, Jessica Coplestone, Jessica Harrison, Jessica Illidge, Jessica Key, Jessica Orr, Jessica Parker, Jessica Roberts, Jill Askin, Jimmy Walsh,

217

Jiorgia Castle, Joanna Sebastien, Jocelyn Bustamante, Jocelyne Martinez, Jodie Lynn, Jodie McDonald, Jodie Shepherd, Jonathan Lin, Jordana Fulker, Josephine Barnes, Joshua Veloso, Julia Len, Julia Urbanowska, Juliann Kelly Son, Julieta Fernandez, Kaede Chiba, Kaira Ford, Kaitlin Dickson, Kaitlin Emery, Kaitlin Orange, Kaitlyn Judd, Kami-Jordan , Karen Richards, Karina KaYu, Karla Higgins, Kat Allen, Kate Abbott, Kate Cyrene Lara, Kate Randell, Kate Richards, Kate Stelfox, Kateland Henderson, Katie Annetts-Smith, Katie Bond, Katie Bridgeman, Katie Cliffe, Katie Concannon, Katie Daly, Katie Jedrek, Katie Morson, Katie Nicholls, Katie Smith, Katie Stanford, Katie Tulip, Katie Wright, Katie Smith, Katrine Widell, Kattiea Devereux-Ward, Katy Goff, Katy Smith, Katy Carswell, Katy Goff, Kay Cera, Kaycee Cool, Kayleigh Anderson Makinson, Kayleigh Andrews, Kayleigh Crowe, Kayleigh Harrison, KC Salangsang, Keeley Lindley, Keisha Waterhouse, Kelly Webb, Kelsey Bell, Kelsey Renton, Kelsie Mai Benson, Kenzy Hegazy, Kerry-Anne Jessop, Kiera Pearson, Kiera McFarlane, Kimberley Roberts, Kirsty Young, Kirsty Wareham-Collins, Kirstyn Lawson, Krystal Z, Kyra Simpson, Lara Macleod, Lara McEwan, Lara Newton, Lara Jade Simpson, Lara Sophie Anna Erdmann, Larissa Thomas, Latisha Anderson, Laura Carwardine, Laura Colman, Laura Gasche, Laura Hurst, Laura Marsh, Laura Mountain, Laura Vocking, Laura-Jane Foxall, Lauren Andrews, Lauren Bradley, Lauren Bryant, Lauren Christopher, Lauren Elvy, Lauren Fee, Lauren Flynn, Lauren Fuller, Lauren Holdstock, Lauren Howard, Lauren King, Lauren McLean, Lauren McManus, Lauren Moore, Lauren Mowat, Lauren Rustage, Lauren Wilford, Lauren-Ashlee Breeden, Laurie Young, Layla Stoneman, Leah Brown, Leah Gill, Leah Gilson-Smith, Leah Haywood, Leah Murray, Leanne Norcup, Lee Beaumont, Leiah Watson, Leighann Demuth, Leilah Boukhedenna, Leona Wilson, Lesley Garside, Lewis Devlin, Libby Harding, Libby Catherine Halford, Liberty E-J, Lila Tasker-Swaffield, Lilian Maybery, Lilly Higgins, Lily Freeman-Skinner, Lilya Taibi, Linde Voldman, Lindsey Bowman, Linthe Weldink, Lis Bird, Lisa Anselmann, Lisa Boisselier, Liv Hawley, Lizzie Graves, Lizzie Smethurst, Lizzy Elson, Lizzy Smart, Lola Boukhedenna, Loraine Gahol, Lore Coolkens, Lorraine Dela Cruz, Louise Dickie, Louise Ridge, Louise Sargent, Louise Michelle Swarbrick, Lucia Maria, Lucie Evans, Lucinda Parsk, Lucy Aitken, Lucy Bartle, Lucy Claydon, Lucy Evans, Lucy Hunter, Lucy M, Lucy Macaulay, Lucy Smith, Lucy Swarbrooke, Lucy Wescombe, Lucy , Lucy Clayton, Lucy Isabella Menaldino, Lydia McMurrie, Lydia O'Boyle, Lydia , Lynette Victoria Ng, Lynne Irish, Mabel Hewitt, Maddie Browne, Maddie Evans, Maddie Knight, Maddie Lloyd, Maddy Reading, Madel Castillo, Madison Corbett, Madison Embury, Madison Gallimore, Mae Thompson-Carse, Maia Gooding, Maiken Jensen, Mairi Hamilton, Maisie Blain, Maisie Ross, Maizey Murrant, Manau Moens, Manjit Seera, Manon Laplante, Manya Satheesha, Marc Cornal, Marcela Masliaev, Maria Martino, María Hidalgo Gómez, Marie Rich, Marjorie Carteret, Mark Lightbown, Marta Sáez Rodríguez, Marta Noelia García Martín, Martina F., Marvin Lagassé, Mary Baker, Marylou Vivier, Mason May, Mathilda Nouali, Matilda Harris, Matilda Pratt, Maxine Withers, Megan Armstrong, Megan Barlett, Megan Burt, Megan Carroll, Megan Eke, Megan Fraser, Megan Joseph, Megan Lane, Megan Molloy, Megan Pannell, Megan Simpson, Megan Smith, Megan Louise Welch, Meghan McCarthy, Mel Simpson, Melike Çörekci, Melissa Riley, Mery Ca, Mharis Leygo, Mia Forbes, Mia Kelly, Michael King, Michela Tosini, Michelle Sandoval, Milla Osborne, Millie Bishop, Millie Jones, Millie Price, Millie Francis, Millie Angel Hunter, Milly Dalton, Miri Kojima, Mirrin Browning, Misha Chaudhry, Mollie Bracewell, Mollie Lewis, Molly Furnell, Molly Jansson, Molly Slack, Molly Dickson, Molly Laidlaww, Morgan Christian, Morgan Evans, Moumita Mandal, Mya Glen, Nadia Andres, Nancy Brodrick, Naow Suwanaklom, Natalie Munro, Natalie Palmer-Bee, Natasha Macdonald, Natasja Silva, Nathalie Stobbe, Neve Orr, Neve Sutherland, Niamh Breen, Niamh Garbutt, Niamh Grant, Niamh Ingram, Niamh Kinsella, Niamh Kitson, Niamh Tait, Niamh O'Donnell, Nicky Richter, Nicola Bowen Jones, Nicola Craig, Nicola Singleton, Nicole Brady, Nicole Currie, Nicole Sardaneta, Nicole H. Caraan, Nikita Saini, Nikki Allen, Nina Verstegen, Nora Hajar Zarmek, Nurin Elyna Emira, Océane Clady, Okamoto Sakura, Olivia Britz, Olivia Lewis, Olivia Muddimer, Olivia Potter, Olivia Humphrey, Olivia Jayne Lynn, Ophelia Hawkeswood, Oran Freeman, Oriana Trommenschlager, Orla Davey, Parichat Mekhanuphak, Paris Drabble, Patrick Kobes, Paula McMenigall, Phoebe Hyde, Phoenix Paterson, Rachael Nulty, Rachael Redford, Rachel Bell, Rachel Brand, Rachel Colven, Rachel Douglas, Rachel Gray, Rachel Hundley, Rachel McCormick, Rachel Oliver, Rachel Saynor, Rachel Schofield, Rachie Sherdley, Rae Preston, Rafaela Magacho, Raini Peeters, Rattanaporn Homlumduan, Rebecca Blaine, Rebecca Galletly, Rebecca Mason, Rebecca Mighty, Rebecca Pawson, Rebecca Phillips, Rebecca Vandenbilcke, Remi Yeh, Renae Banfield, Rhiane Cuthill, Rhiannah McCourt, Ria Walker, Rianna Fry, Rianna Wolton, Ricard Mateu, Riley Haworth, Ro Cantelli, Rob Bradley, Roberta Ghione, Rocha Gould, Rocío Sevillano, Romane Cosson, Romina Macol, Rosy Zuccherino, Ryan Clements, Ryan Wilks, Sadie Mosley, Safeeya Kazi, Saira Naisbitt, Samantha Herron, Samantha Hughes, Samantha Pilling, Samantha Roberts, Samia Alisha, Sandra Gijsbers, Sandra Sjöberg, Sara Demontis, Sarah Christie, Sarah Ling, Sarah McFadyen, Sarah Pritchett, Sarah Sturrock, Sasha Dale, Scarlet Nation, Serena Ömrüm Taşdöğen, Serene Arnold, Shan Bayley, Shannon Cusack, Shannon Hutchinson, Shannon McNamara, Sharna O'Brien, Sharon Moran, Shauna Bertram, Shauna Cox, Shellie Chacon, Sierra Chavez, Sinead Bullers, Sinead O'Donnell, Siobhan Hannon, Skye Elizabeth Zora Broad, Sofi Moreira, Sofia King, Sofia Bella Esposito, Sol Loredo, Sophia Jones, Sophie Beach, Sophie Bull, Sophie Canner, Sophie Dight, Sophie Embleton, Sophie Grant, Sophie Grigg, Sophie Haddon, Sophie Hay, Sophie Hughes, Sophie Hutson, Sophie Jones, Sophie Royle-Hughes, Sophie Toms, Sorcha Connellan, Stacey Albon, Stefhani Chan Jacik, Steph Kidd, Stephanie Donnelly, Stephanie Howlett, Stephanie Waldron, Stephanie Alden-Barrett, Stuart Leslie, Suman Cheema, Susan Tiong, Susanna Shields, Suwanaklom , Suzanne Dinsmore, Sydney Evans, Sydney Sheppard, Sylvia Hiam, Sylvia Mower, Tady O'Toole, Tammy Dingle, Tamsin Williams, Tash Marshall, Teresa Minahan, Thia Hough, Tianna Gray, Tianne Takayesu, Tiegan Ward, Tiffani Broomfield, Tiffany Barratt, Tiffany Yim, Tilly Agnew, Tomás Dyson, Tomisin Fijabi, Toni Brown, Tonicha Coulthard, Tracey Demelo, Tracy Laurence, Valentine Parrinello, Vera Taskaya, Verónica van Bommel Villaroel, Vickie McKenzie, Victoria Joyce, Victoria Zúñiga-López, Violett Spear, Vitória Arenari, Vivian Boehnke, Wendy Ilona, Wilke Van Den Berg, Willemijn Mooij, Willow Mason, Yasmin Bates, Yin-Ting Tang, Yioula Ellina, Zara Morgan-Glass, Zinnia Claire Seno, Zoe Quinton